上海市I类高峰学科（外国语言文学）建设项目成果

Supported by Shanghai Peak Discipline (Class 1):
Foreign Language and Literature

U0783605

◎跨文化视角下的中国：

外国专家的中国文化故事

——— 第一辑 ———

A CROSS-CULTURAL
PERSPECTIVE ON CHINA:
FOREIGN EXPERTS' CHINESE
CULTURAL STORIES

张红玲　主编

上海外语教育出版社
外教社 SHANGHAI FOREIGN LANGUAGE EDUCATION PRESS

图书在版编目（CIP）数据

跨文化视角下的中国：外国专家的中国文化故事. 第1辑/张红玲主编.
—上海：上海外语教育出版社，2016
ISBN 978-7-5446-4521-8

I. ①跨… II. ①张… III. ①中外关系—文化交流—文集—汉、英
IV. ①G125-53

中国版本图书馆CIP数据核字(2016)第235404号

出版发行：上海外语教育出版社

（上海外国语大学内）　邮编：200083
电　　　话：021-65425300（总机）
电子邮箱：bookinfo@sflep.com.cn
网　　　址：http://www.sflep.com.cn　http://www.sflep.com
责任编辑：梁瀚杰

印　　刷：上海叶大印务发展有限公司
开　　本：890×1240　1/32　印张 6.75　字数 183千字
版　　次：2016 年 12 月第 1 版　2016 年 12 月第 1 次印刷
印　　数：2 100 册

书　　号：ISBN 978-7-5446-4521-8 / G·1452
定　　价：23.00 元

本版图书如有印装质量问题，可向本社调换

目 录

Contents

前　言

　　十五年前，我作为富布赖特学者在美国明尼苏达大学研修，在明尼阿波利斯这个美国中西部城市生活了近一年。作为一名跨文化研究学者，这一年对我来说既是学习和研究的一年，也是跨文化探索和实践的一年，可谓成果丰硕，感悟深刻。记得我有一个美国朋友，她年过五旬，事业有成，家庭幸福，当时刚辞去工作，回到学校攻读硕士学位。我们有共同修读的课程，经常一起上课、学习，于是便成为朋友。我经常受邀到她家做客，与她和她丈夫非常熟悉。他们善良、热情，喜欢阅读。然而，在多次闲聊过程中，我惊讶地发现他们对中国的了解相当有限，甚至偏颇。在他们看来，我远离丈夫和孩子，独自一人在美国生活学习，不可思议，"这就是'红色中国'只讲革命、不讲人权的一个例证。"我回国后不久，邀请他们来上海旅游。他们从踏进我家大门那一刻起就接连发出惊讶和感叹："啊，你们家竟然用的是木地板，有钢琴，还有鲜花！"在他们的印象里，中国还停留在封建、专制、落后的时代，普通百姓的生活怎么可能如此讲究！

　　由此，一个问题时时缠绕在我心头：为什么很多美国人对中国的理解与我们的期待如此大相径庭？他们对中国的刻板印象如何才能改变？

　　经过三十多年的改革开放，中国已经发展成为世界第二大经济体。随着国力的不断增强，世界期待中国承担更多国际责任，中国也希望在促进世界各国、各民族、各文化之间的沟通理解、交流互鉴方面起到更加积极的推动作用。十八大以来，习近平主席在多次出访演讲中积极倡导构建人类命运共同体，合作共赢和命运共同体成为我国对外交往的重要理念。"一带一路"和亚投行等战略举措，就是这些理念的具体体现。

人文交流与心灵相通，是实现合作共赢、构建命运共同体的重要保证。每个文化都有其发展环境和历史渊源，具有各自的特点，人类文明因此而丰富多彩。中国文化源远流长，博大精深。正如习近平主席所说："观察和认识中国，历史和现实都要看，物质和精神也都要看。中华民族5000多年文明史，中国人民近代以来170多年斗争史，中国共产党90多年奋斗史，中华人民共和国60多年发展史，改革开放30多年探索史，这些历史一脉相承，不可割裂。脱离了中国的历史，脱离了中国的文化，脱离了中国人的精神世界，脱离了当代中国的深刻变革，是难以正确认识中国的。"习总书记还强调，"要精心做好对外宣传工作，创新对外宣传方式，着力打造融通中外的新概念新范畴新表述，讲好中国故事，传播好中国声音。"

综上所述，如何让世界了解中国、认识中国，如何传播中国文化，讲述中国故事，这是一项意义重大又极具挑战的任务，是一个值得研究的课题。通常我们更关注的是，如何通过政府机构、文化组织、非政府组织、教育机构等有意识的组织行为，去进行中国文化的介绍和传播。近年来，随着公共外交理念不断推广，公众参与文化交流和传播的积极性越来越高。这些可以概括为中国文化传播的"走出去"模式。

让世界了解中国的另一个有效途径是"请进来"，即充分发挥留学生和在华旅游、工作的外籍人士的作用。这里包含两个层面的意义：第一，在华外籍学生和工作人员可以将他们在中国的亲身经历与感受带回国，与国人分享；第二，他们对中国的印象反馈给我们，有助于我们更好地认识自我，完善自我。

上海外国语大学作为一所国际化水平较高的大学，每年聘请来自世界30余个国家的百余名专家来校任教或从事科学研究。他们或在上海短期停留（一个月至三个月），或长期生活（半年至一年，甚至十余年）。他们的足迹不仅集中于课堂、学校，出于对中国和中国文化的兴趣，他们常常会在工作之余，利用节假日去上海的大街小巷，去中国的东南西北、城市乡村，走走看看。以他们的视角来审视中国，一定会给我们带来新的发现。

"我的文化故事"是上海外国语大学跨文化研究中心教学团队自上世纪90年代以来，在"跨文化交际"课程中一直坚持的一项学习任务，来自世界各地修读本课程的学生都必须完成这项作业，目的是让学生回顾和反思自己的人生经历，记录和讲述让自己印象深刻或产生重要影响的跨文化经历，同时通过与其他同学分享、交流各自的文化故事，达到增强跨文化意识、提升跨文化能力的目的。

"外国专家的中国文化故事"项目借鉴"跨文化交际"课程教学的经验，利用外国专家在华生活和工作的机会，请他们讲述自己的中国文化故事，以期从中发现他们对中国的关注点，了解他们眼中的中国。实际上，高校外国专家群体素质高、有思想，他们来中国除了教学科研之外，本来就有探索中国、了解中国的希望。当我校的外国专家了解这个项目时，大都表现出极高的热情和参与愿望。因此，征稿通知发出仅四个月，我们就收到了30位专家的来稿。这些稿件内容丰富，形式各异。体裁方面，有散文、小说、诗歌、演讲等。稿件内容涉猎广泛，有历史、哲学、语言、文学、美食、旅游等。有的从宏观角度出发，纵论古今，横贯中外；有的从微观小事入手，以个体的细腻笔触，描绘自己在中国工作和生活的心路历程；有的对中国经济的飞速发展表示惊叹、赞美，也有的对中国社会的不良现象提出批评。撰稿外教中，少数人刚到中国数月，尚处于各种新鲜事物的感官"轰炸"之中，因而笔下的叙述更多的是对中国的"第一印象"；而更多的撰稿者在中国工作生活已有数年，个别甚至已经在中国结婚生子，会说流利的汉语，对中国的熟悉早已超出看"西洋镜"或会讲"上海话"的层面，因而他们笔下的中国又是另一番图景。

由于这些外国专家来自世界各地，每个人的文化及家庭背景、教育情况、宗教信仰、价值观往往迥异，加上他们独特的人生经历，导致他们看待事物的角度非常多元化。尽管如此，大多数外国人在中国生活和工作一段时间以后，都会达成一个共识，即中国文化之博大精深，中国社会之错综复杂，中国发展之天翻地覆，绝不是一个外国人一朝一夕就能真正理解领悟的，而这其中的矛盾和不确定性也恰恰是生活在中国的挑战和乐趣所在。援引一位法国专家在《解读中国》一文中的话："……法国正在日益变成一个停滞不前、自我封闭、对外来人愈加严苛的国家。法国可预见的、洁净的和标准化的舒适生活很容易麻痹人的感官……相反，中国却让你的感官觉醒，让你感到自己是活着的，它强迫你去感受。中国人有一种'万事皆有可能'的心态，而当今的法国人却变得日益悲观消极。中国是生机盎然的，而法国却在沉睡。对有些外国人来说，中国实在有点难以消化。但对我来说，每天的感官刺激让我能保持清醒和活力。对很多外国人来说，他们对中国的感情是爱恨交织。对我来说，它是连绵不断的喧闹、矛盾和变化，当我不在中国时，就会想念这一切。随着在中国生活的时间越来越长，我发现自己对中国的理解和认知也日渐加深，同样，我的困惑也越来越多，但我已经逐渐学会用泰然处之的心态面对它们。"

这位来自欧洲的外国专家道出了很多在华外国人的心声。事实上，我们在与外国人打交道的过程中常会发现，那些对中国文化抱有强烈好奇心、乐于发现并探索新鲜事物、敢于走出自我心理舒适区（comfort zone）、勇于尝试的外国人，往往更容易适应当地环境；反之，那些不愿意敞开心胸、抗拒接触或理解当地文化的外国人往往有着很糟糕的文化体验。令人欣慰的是，我们从绝大多数外国专家的来稿中感受到的是前者：他们努力学习汉语和中国文化，积极扩大社交圈子，兴致勃勃地品尝中国美食，前往中国各地体验当地的风土人情。尽管他们在中国免不了遇到挫败和不快，但总体来说，在中国工作、生活的经历对他们来说绝对是独一无二、永生难忘的。

在当今全球化的背景下，越来越多的人离开故乡，选择"生活在别处"。"不识庐山真面目，只缘身在此山中。"作为中国人，我们对身边的一切早已习以为常，感官趋于迟钝。而这些外国人既在"山外"，又在"山中"，他们充满感性的、对我们长期忽视的细节的重新发现也因此显得更加有趣和弥足珍贵。此书最大的价值，或许不是这群外国人在中国工作、生活的点滴，而在于，从他们那里，我们会发现还有一个我们不熟悉、不了解的"别样中国"。

《跨文化视角下的中国》是一套外国人讲述中国故事、传播中国文化的系列丛书，得到了上海外国语大学I类高峰学科（外国语言文学）建设项目的资助。

参与本书组稿、编辑和翻译的人员包括：

组稿：张红玲、张赟、梁晓雪

编辑：张红玲、林帜

翻译：George Fleming（费祖志）、梁晓雪等

上海外国语大学小语种专业的师生为其外国专家的作品提供了小语种翻译服务。上海外语教育出版社的梁瀚杰作为责任编辑为本书的策划和定稿提出了想法，贡献了智慧。对他们的付出，在此谨致以衷心的感谢。

张红玲

2016年8月

PREFACE

Fifteen years ago, I studied at the University of Minnesota as a Fulbright Scholar, living in Minneapolis for almost a year. As a researcher of cross-cultural studies, that year was for me about learning and research as well as an opportunity to put my theories about cross-cultural studies to practice. I gained many insights from my time in Minneapolis. There was an American friend of mine in her fifties, who had a successful career and happy family life. She had just resigned from her job and returned to academia to pursue a Master's degree. We shared certain courses and often went to class or studied together, becoming friends. She often invited me to her home; I grew close to her and her husband. They were kind, warm people, and avid readers. However, after many conversations I realized that they had a very limited, even skewed, picture of China. They could not understand my decision to leave behind my husband and child to study in America alone — for them it was "proof that 'Red China' was interested only in revolution and not human rights." Not long after I returned to China, I invited them to Shanghai on holiday. The moment they stepped in to my home, they were gasping nonstop in amazement: "What? You actually have a wooden floor, a piano and fresh flowers!"

The China of their imagination was a country stuck in the feudal, autocratic, backwards era, where the ordinary people could not possibly afford such luxuries. After that, I was frustrated by a question: why was so many Americans' understanding of China so skewed from what we Chinese had hoped? How could stereotypes be changed?

After more than three decades of economic and political reform, China has become the world's second largest economy. With increased international influence, the international community hopes that China will take on more responsibility internationally. Meanwhile, China also desires to play a more active role in creating understanding and learning between countries, nations and cultures around the world. Since the 18th CPC National Congress, President Xi Jinping has on numerous visits abroad emphasized the necessity for mankind to see its symbiotic destiny. This and cooperation for mutual benefit have become an important part of Chinese diplomacy. The "One Belt One Road" initiative, the AIIB and other strategic measures have put into practice these diplomatic ideals.

Bringing together individuals and minds is an important way to ensure success in mutual benefit cooperation and symbiotic destiny. Each culture has developed against a particular environment and historical context, and has its own distinct character. This has allowed human civilization to become as rich and varied as it is. Chinese culture is both ancient and profound. To quote President Xi, "Observing and understanding China requires a knowledge of both history and the present, of the material as well as the spiritual. Chinese history is unbroken, from the beginning of the Chinese civilization over five millennia ago, through the struggles of the Chinese people over the past 170 years, the endeavors of the Communist Party of China over the past 90 years, the development of the People's Republic of China over the past 60 years, and the explorations of Reform and Opening Up of the past three decades. A proper understanding of China is incomplete without understanding Chinese history, culture, the spiritual realm of its people, and the profound changes the country has undergone."

Xi Jinping has also emphasized that "China needs to make significant efforts in promoting itself globally, using innovative new methods. Our country needs to focus on combining Chinese and international ideas and expressions, in order to tell the story of China and make China's voice heard."

In summary, to tell the Chinese story by improving international understanding of China and promoting traditional Chinese culture is an extremely important but challenging task, and one worthy of study. In the past, there has been a focus on conscious, organized efforts by government, cultural groups, NGOs, and educational institutions to inform about and promote Chinese culture. In recent years, with growing recognition of the importance of public diplomacy, the public has played an increasingly central role in cultural transmission. These developments can be summarized as the "Going

Global" move in Chinese culture.

Another effective means to inform the world about China is to "invite" the world in. This refers to the role played by international students, tourists and foreign workers in China. This group is important for two reasons. Firstly, international students and professionals in our country can relate their experiences in China to their compatriots back home. Secondly, by informing us of their impressions, we can gain another perspective on ourselves and improve.

As an elite institution that is comparatively open to the outside world, Shanghai International Studies University (SISU) recruits about 200 foreign experts from more than 30 countries around the world each year to teach or undertake research. Some of them stay for shorter periods (one to three months), while others stay here for the long term (half a year to a year, or even more than a decade). They leave their mark not only in the classroom and around the university: because of their interest in our country and its culture, in addition to the duties of their work, they often explore the snaking alleyways of Shanghai; travel around the country; and see both urban and rural areas. China viewed from their perspective is surely instructive for us.

"China in My Eyes" began as a task in the Cross-Cultural Communication course at Shanghai International Studies University's Center for Cross-Cultural Research in the 1990s. Students on this course from all over the world have been required to complete this task, with a view to getting them to reflect on their experiences, and to record those events which had a particularly strong impact on them cross-culturally. Furthermore, by sharing their experiences with those around them and learning about those of their peers, these students gain a better understanding of cross-cultural experience and learn about adapting in different cultural contexts.

Inspired by the Cross-Cultural Communication course, the "China in My Eyes" project asks foreign experts working and living in China to share their China stories, in order to discover issues of particular relevance and see our country from their point of view. These university-employed foreign experts are of a high caliber, are idealists, and have come to China not just to pursue teaching and research but also to learn about our country. When SISU's foreign experts learned about our project, the vast majority expressed a keen willingness to take part. This is how, in just four months after we issued a call for submissions, we received 30 essays from our international faculty. These stories cover a wide range of topics and forms. They include prose, novels, poetry, and speeches, covering (amongst other topics) history, philosophy, language, literature, cuisine and travel. Some contributions take a macroscopic view, taking a broad look at China's history and development and its interaction with other countries; others focus on a particular experience, seeking through intricate personal stories to describe the experience of work and life in China. Others still remark with wonder and praise at the pace of development in our country, or provide some criticisms of the less positive aspects of our society.

Of those international faculty who submitted contributions,

some had only been in our country several months, still overwhelmed by a sensory bombardment, which means that their
stories are like a first impression of China. A larger number of
essays have been written by those who have lived and worked
in China for several years, some of whom have even married
and started families here and who speak fluent Chinese. For
this reason, their understanding of our country is more nu-
anced than simple stereotypes or attempts to speak Shanghainese.

These international faculty members come from all over the
world. Each individual has a different culture, family back-
ground, level of education, faith, and set of values. Coupled
with their unique experiences, they have an immense scope
of different perspectives between them. Nevertheless, having
lived and worked in China for a time, the great majority of foreigners will agree on the richness of Chinese culture, the com-
plexity of its society, and the tremendous change sweeping the
nation. These are not something that an individual foreigner
can comprehend in a short space of time; the complications
and uncertainties in our country form a part of the challenge
and pleasure of the Chinese experience. To quote a French expert in "Making Sense of China": "To me, France is becoming
increasingly stagnant, closed on itself, intolerant towards non-
Europeans. As opposed to the predictable, sanitized, standardized comfort of France which tames my senses (I will admit
an exception for the cheese and wine), China awakens your
senses and makes you feel alive, it forces you to have feelings. Chinese people have an attitude that makes everything

seem possible, while the French are nowadays pessimistic and resigned. China is alive and France is asleep. For some foreigners this is just too much to take in, but for me this daily thrill keeps me awake and alive. For many foreigners their relationship with China is a love-hate relationship. For me it is the constant buzz, changes and contradictions described above that I miss when I am not in China. As I spend more time in China, I find myself gaining understanding and becoming more knowledgeable, yet growing increasingly confused and at ease with this confusion."

This European foreign expert's words will resonate with many international residents in China. When we work with foreigners, we discover that those with a passionate curiosity for Chinese culture, who are willing to explore new things, and who are willing to step outside their comfort zone, are often better at adapting to their new environment. By contrast, those unwilling to broaden their horizons, or refuse to connect with or understand Chinese culture, tend to have a less positive experience. Fortunately, the vast majority of our international faculty belong to the former group: they endeavour to learn Chinese and about our culture, getting involved socially, trying Chinese food, and travelling all over the country to experience the local cultures. Despite the inevitability of difficulties or gripes, most of their China experience is unique and unforgettably positive.

Against the backdrop of globalization, ever more people are leaving their hometowns behind and choosing to live elsewhere. To quote the Song dynasty poet Su Dongpo, "I cannot see what Mt. Lu looks like really, because I am standing there." Having grown up with them, we Chinese have dulled our senses to our surroundings. These foreigners, however, can both stand "on", and "at a distance from" the mountain, thus gaining a clearer picture. Their sensitive rediscovery of details overlooked by us for so long is therefore all the more fascinating and precious. The greatest value of this book lies perhaps not so much in the details of each foreigner's China experience, but in how we can discover "another" China that we do not know or understand.

A Cross-cultural Perspective on China is a book series dedicated to foreigners in China sharing cultural stories and communicating the Chinese culture. It is listed as one of the projects under the Peak Discipline (Foreign Language and Literature) Development Program.

For this volume, the editing and translating team consists of the following members:

Project designer: Zhang Hongling

Soliciting contributions: Zhang Hongling, Zhang Yun, Liang Xiaoxue

Editing: Zhang Hongling, Lin Zhi

Translation: George Fleming, Liang Xiaoxue

Teachers and students from less-commonly-taught language departments of Shanghai International Studies University helped translate their foreign teachers' articles into English or Chinese. Mr. Liang Hanjie, a very talented and responsible editor of Shanghai Foreign Language Education Press, has also offered his valuable suggestions for the designing of this book series. To all of the above-mentioned people, I wish to extend my sincere gratitude.

Zhang Hongling

August 2016 in Shanghai

一、观察篇

CHINA AND I

Ana Filipa Teixeira Rodrigues Ferreira Teles

It was at the close of 2010 that I found out I would be coming to live in Shanghai. Before that, I had never imagined the idea. That year, China and Shanghai were all over the news in Portugal because of the 2010 World Expo. Coverage of the region had been gradually intensifying over the years, ever since the Beijing Olympics. These two great events have also meant that now, you often hear the Portuguese talk about China. However, the China we read about in the papers, magazines or see on television is not the country most of us imagine. China in the popular Portuguese imagination is a country with a long and tangled history with Portugal; it is also the version I remember. Christmas Day 2010 was the last Christmas I spent in Portugal before I arrived in Shanghai. My family gave me a travel guide to the country which introduced all the provinces and included a map and photographs. As I turned each page, I felt excitement and anticipation in my fingertips. The strangeness of the photographs really caught me by surprise. Months before I actually arrived in China, I had already begun to roam the country.

I have always harboured a fascination for the "East." I think many Portuguese feel similarly to myself. Ours is an ancient country — extremely ancient. Half of her history is intertwined with the East. In 1498 Vasco da Gama arrived in India. A few years later, in 1513, the Portuguese reached China. From that point onwards, our fate was entwined with that of the Middle Kingdom, which was even more ancient than our own. Growing up, our study of history was a series of stories of navigators, their sea voyages and interactions with foreign peoples, as well as the wealth they brought back with them to Lisbon from the East. Like Shanghai today, Lisbon in the 16th century was an international port where goods and people from all over the world passed through. The Portuguese brought pearls, silk, tea and ceramics from China. At the same time, Queen Catherine of England (originally from Braganza, Portugal) introduced tea to the English court, establishing it as part of court custom. It was from that point onwards that the elegant tradition of afternoon tea began to sweep the globe.

At my parents' house, we used to drink jasmine tea from a Chinese tea set. I grew up there surrounded by Chinese elements that had come via Mozambique, where my parents lived for a time and which before 1974 had a large Chinese expat population. At home we had mah-jong, chopsticks, a Chinese tea set, and other Chinese things. All of these were purchased in Mozambique, Portugal's ancient colony, and are still at my parents' house. However, today they have a more profound meaning for me because my personal experiences in China have allowed me to understand what they represent.

I have been in China for almost four years and this Christmas is my fourth here, far from my country and family, and far away from the bustling festive atmosphere in Lisbon's streets. The past four years have been testing but amazing for me. They're like four pearls. Every year, I overcome difficulties and gain career and life experience, and these fuse into a dazzling, perfectly round pearl.

Over the past four years, I have travelled all over China, to many different provinces and cities. I have become more familiar with Chinese food, festivals, culture and society. China has a rich, complex and diverse culture that would take several lifetimes to understand properly. As I look through the guide I was given back then, I recognize many of the places in the pictures, and can say the names of the cities and provinces. Those images are no longer strange to me. I can now say, and believe with certainty, that the cultures of our two nations are not so unlike, because we are all people. This is the tie that binds us together and bridges the gaps in ethnicity, geography, language and race, overcoming all barriers and divisions of thought.

I have had many experiences over the past four years. It's difficult to do justice to all the ways in which I love China. Its traditional culture is fascinating; every time I read the poetry of Li Bai or Du Fu, I am touched deeply by the excellence of their art. Even several hundred years later, and translated from ancient Chinese to modern Portuguese, each poem is still just as palpably elegant. I am also a great fan of tea culture. Now, I know my tea, and how to brew a cup in the proper Chinese way. I like a pot of green tea or Pu'er while listening to the Chinese zither or Erhu. I wish I could take a journey in one of the sailboats of the age of navigators, a boat full of treasures from China on a course for Lisbon. I could then found my own, small Chinese museum, full of jewels, ceramics, scrolls, makeup and fans.

Four years later, I can truly appreciate the China that was presented to the Portuguese viewer at the Shanghai Expo in 2010. The images on display were those of contemporary China as it really is — parts of it even more modern than little Portugal, nestled as it is at the western tip of Europe. Over these few years, the relations between our two countries have grown closer, while large-scale Chinese investments in Portugal have changed perceptions of China in my country.

My time in China has been a wonderful experience, full of precious memories, both those happy and tinged with sadness. Like I say, every year here produces a pearl that stays with me as I continue to grow and discover a new me, different from my old self. Many of my ancestors have travelled to China, whether to Macau or the mainland, to develop trade or new congregations for the church. Camoes, Portugal's greatest poet, and Bocage, the romantic poet, are both said to have visited China. There are many others as well, although their names are fading from memory. 2014 was the 400th anniversary of the publishing of Fernao Mendes Pinto's *Pilgrimage*, which records the first encounters between the Portuguese and the peoples of the Far East.

Portugal is a small country at the western tip of the European continent, bathed in the cool, blue waters of the Atlantic. I often think about those azure waves from my post in Shanghai. I think there will certainly come a day when I return to that blue coast, touched by the breeze — my motherland and home that remains at the depths of my heart. I will fly over the Eurasian continent. Lisbon, set as it is at the other end of the Silk Road, awaits. The ancient port was once crowded with triple-mast carracks laden with riches from the east. I will return there, taking all the precious experiences that living in China has given me over the years.

It's now December. Shanghai is cold and clammy; the sky is overcast. It's colder than Lisbon but not as grey. Another year has passed and China is preparing for its New Year celebrations. From my house in China, I can see the dark sky over Shanghai. In the distance shines the Oriental Pearl tower; the famous skyscrapers in Pudong are all lit up. On such a cold, dark night, those flickering lights are like the little ones on a Christmas tree. I look outside once again and see Shanghai bathed in white moonlight, while I seem to hear the poet Li Bai's words in my ear:

Moonlight outside my window,
Or is it frost on the ground?
I look up to the bright moon,
Then look down, sick for home.

About the author:

Ana Filipa Teixeira Rodrigues Ferreira Teles (Portuguese) studied teaching of Portuguese as a second language at Lisbon University. She taught Portuguese from March 2011 to August 2015 at the School of European and Latin American Studies (SELAS), SISU.

中国与我

Ana Filipa Teixeira Rodrigues Ferreira Teles（葡萄牙）

　　我是在2010年年底得知自己将要来上海的。在那之前，我从未想过自己会来上海。那一年，由于上海世博会的举办，很多关于中国、关于上海的消息传到了葡萄牙。其实从北京奥运会之后，关于中国的新闻就开始日渐频繁地进入我们的视野。也正因为这两大盛事，在葡萄牙经常能听到人们谈论中国。只不过，我们通过报纸、杂志、电视看到的画面并非是我们大家想象中的中国。想象中的她历史悠久，还与葡萄牙有不解之缘，而那也曾是我记忆中的中国。2010年12月25日是我来上海前在葡萄牙度过的最后一个圣诞节，我的家人送给我一本中国旅游指南，书里有所有的省份，有地图，还有照片。我一页页翻阅着，指尖溢满了喜悦和期待，书中的照片是那样的奇异，出乎我的意料。手拿着那本指南，我在抵达上海之前数月，就已经开始了我的中国之旅。

我一直迷恋东方，或许很多葡萄牙人跟我有着类似的情愫。葡萄牙是一个古老的国度，非常的古老，而它一半的历史都叙写着它和东方的情结。1498年，航海家达伽马到达了印度。不久之后的1513年，葡萄牙人来到了中国。从那以后，葡萄牙的命运开始与"中心之国"连结，这是一个比葡萄牙更为古老的国度。求学期间，伴随着我们成长的，是航海家、航海旅程以及接触他国人民的一系列故事，以及他们从东方带到里斯本的财富。正如现在的上海，里斯本在16世纪曾是一个国际港口，那里穿梭着来自全世界的财富和各类人等。从中国，葡萄牙人带去了珍珠、丝绸、茶叶和瓷器。而从葡萄牙，来自布拉干萨的英格兰和苏格兰王后唐娜·卡塔琳娜将茶引入了英国宫廷，使之在宫廷习俗中"制度化"。自那而后，喝"下午茶"这一高贵的习惯风靡全球。

在我父母家，我们用中国的茶具品尝茉莉花茶。我的父母曾在莫桑比克住过一段时间，莫桑比克是葡萄牙以前的殖民地，1974年之前还有很多中国侨民。我父母在莫桑比克买了麻将、筷子和一套中国瓷器，还有其他一些中国的东西，这些东西现在还在我父母家里。这些中国元素伴随了我的成长，但如今，它们对我而言更加意义深远，因为通过自己在中国的切身经历，我更能理解它们的含义。

我到中国已经快四年了。今年是我第四次在中国过圣诞节，远离家乡，与节日气氛浓厚的里斯本街头相隔千里。过去的这艰苦而又奇妙的四年，于我而言，就如同四粒珍珠一般。每一年，在克服了困难、丰富了职业和生活阅历之后，都凝结成一颗完美夺目、玉润浑圆的珍珠。

　　四年间，我游历中国，到过很多的省份和城市，对中国美食、节日、文化和社会也更为熟悉。中国文化博大精深、丰富多元，我不知要活几世才能彻底了解。如今，翻阅着四年前圣诞节收到的那本旅游指南，我能认出很多的图片，说出城市和省份的名字。看着那些照片，它们对我来说也已不再奇异。现在，我可以说，并且也坚定地相信，中葡两国文化并非迥异，因为我们都是人，而正是这一纽带，能让我们紧密联系在一起，超越民族、地域、语言和种族的差异，冲破一切阻隔和思想的界限。

　　过去的四年我经历了很多，实难尽数中国让我喜爱之处。中国的传统文化如此迷人，每每阅读李白和杜甫的诗歌，那份艺术的精致都深深触动我心。尽管已过去数个世纪，尽管由古汉语译成了当代葡文，但字里行间，我们还是能感受到优美高雅的诗情意韵。我也非常欣赏茶文化。现在我能够区分茶的种类，也能按照中国文化习惯沏茶。我喜欢品一壶绿茶或是普洱，我喜欢听一曲古筝或是二胡。我多希望能乘着航海时代的帆船，满载中国的宝藏驶回里斯本，建立一个属于我的、小小的中国博物馆，珍宝荟萃，尽是瓷器、画卷、妆奁和古扇。

　　四年后的今天，我全然体会了2010年上海世博会期间呈现在葡萄牙眼前的中国印象。那些都是当代中国的真实写照，有时甚至远比我那小小的、静卧在欧洲最西端的祖国显得更为现代。这四年来，中葡关系日益紧密，中国在葡萄牙的大量投资也使葡萄牙人对中国的感观有所改变。

　　在中国生活是一段奇妙的经历，珍贵的记忆满溢，丰载着欢笑，亦偶有唏嘘。正如我所说，在中国的每一年都蕴成一颗珍珠，伴我不断积淀，发现不同以往的自己。为了开拓贸易，或是为了传播教义，许多葡萄牙先辈曾在中国留下足迹——在澳门，或是内地。葡萄牙最伟大的诗人卡蒙斯，还有浪漫主义诗人博卡热，据说都曾来过这里，还有更多其他人，尽管他们的名字已难记起。2014年，大家还纪念了费尔南·门德斯·平托的《远游记》这本记录葡萄牙人与东方人最初往来的作品出版400周年。

葡萄牙是欧洲大陆最西端的一个小国，沐浴着碧蓝透凉的大西洋海水。身在上海的我，常常遥想那一片碧波荡漾，想着终有一天，我会回到那轻风拂面的蓝色海岸——那是深藏在我脑海中的祖国家园。我将飞翔在亚欧大陆的上空。而里斯本，就在这丝绸之路的另一端盼望着我的归去。那个古老的港口，曾经停靠着满载东方财富的三桅帆船。我也将回到那里，带着这些年在中国的生活留给我的珍贵经历。

现在是十二月，上海气候阴冷，天色灰沉；比里斯本更冷，却又没那么灰沉。又一年过去了，中国即将欢度新春佳节。我在中国的家里，透过窗户，看到上海夜色深沉。远处，东方明珠灯光闪耀，浦东其他著名的高楼也灯火通明。在寒冷的黑夜里，灯光闪烁发亮，就像是葡萄牙圣诞树上的小灯。我又一次将目光投向窗外，皎洁的月色照着上海，而我的耳边，仿佛响起了李白的诗句：

床前明月光，
疑是地上霜。
举头望明月，
低头思故乡。

作者简介：

Ana Filipa Teixeira Rodrigues Ferreira Teles（葡萄牙籍）毕业于新里斯本大学对外葡语教学专业，于2011年3月至2015年8月期间担任上海外国语大学西方语学院葡萄牙语系教师。

SHANGHAI, AS I SEE IT

Eni Karlieni

Shanghai is one of China's most famous cities, with a long history and rich culture of its own, sitting beside where the Yangtze River enters the East China Sea. Shanghai is famous as the country's largest industrialized city and port. As a metropolis, Shanghai's infrastructure and facilities are developing all the time. High-rise apartments and highways tower over the city; transport is convenient; labyrinths of tunnels snake under the ground; and there are busy shopping malls everywhere. Everything is geared towards the needs of the city.

Most of Shanghai's residents live in flats, with the city's 5,800km^2 home to 25 million people. The burgeoning of the population has led to inevitable imbalances in the city's development. From the plain to the state of the art, from the cheap to the expensive, more and more apartments are being constructed in the city. Of course, the style and price of a flat depend on how well furnished it is.

Shanghai's metro is the most popular form of public transport. Apart from the metro, people take the bus. The metro takes passengers in every direction to almost every place imaginable. Tickets are reasonably priced, and the service is pretty fast. However, at certain times, especially during the commute rush hour, there's little hope of getting a seat because the carriages are packed with passengers. Even so, the metro is still a better way to get around than owning a car; there is no issue of congestion.

The highway system is the infrastructure on which the transport industry rests. The sky above is crisscrossed with intersections five or more storeys high and stretching in every direction. The road system isn't just going upwards; it is spreading underground too. Just like the intersections above, there are many levels of tunnels below; it's fantastic!

The city has all sorts of attractions. There are shopping malls that stretch from the basement to the sky; there is natural scenery, both in the city centre and in the suburbs; and as for good food, there is everything from the traditional to the modern, from the cheap to the pricey. All of these are developing apace with that of the country as a whole.

On Nanjing Road and Huaihai Road are malls catering to those of a higher social status or the better off. These malls sell famous brands like Louis Vuitton, Cartier, Hermès, Aigner, Chloe, and Coach. Still, don't bother going to these shops unless you have very deep pockets, because the items on sale are very dear indeed. Crowds of people pass by, either buying or just window shopping the clothes, bags, shoes and electronics on sale. There are red lanterns decorated with Chinese characters along Nanjing Road. In the run up to Christmas, the streets and shops are festooned with Christmas decorations.

For those of us on a low to middle income, there are some large shopping malls like Hongkou Plaza, or ones at People's Square or Zhongshan Park, but it's more interesting to visit the Yu Garden, the Shanghai Science & Technology Museum or Qipu Road.

The Yu Garden is a fascinating place. There are traditional Chinese buildings and an ancient garden with a towering wall, the Jade Garden. It is designed in a slightly different way to the traditional gardens of the Far East, with upturned eaves and cornices on its buildings and painted mainly in red and gold. The garden dates from the Ming Dynasty (1368-1644 CE). Nearby are many different malls selling every sort of jade or other precious gemstone. These are typically Chinese souvenirs that make good presents. The price is relative to the item and depends on how good quality the consumer wants. The price is also not always fixed; you can haggle for some products, not for others.

Those looking to buy clothing, bags, shoes, all kinds of souvenirs, scarves, knitted tablecloths or pearls can visit the Shanghai Science & Technology Museum. There aren't too many visitors and there's a comfortable atmosphere. Most of the visitors are foreigners. The products are extremely expensive. You have to be a good haggler and get the price down to half that offered. There's a special way to manage it: don't be in too much of a hurry to haggle. Instead, walk away until the shopkeeper calls you back. If they don't, that means the price they were offering is a low one.

Qipu Road is good for buying things at a reasonable price. It's a really busy shopping centre. People come from everywhere to shop here because Qipu is a wholesale exchange place; the majority of people there are businessmen. Qipu has all kinds of products like bags, clothing for infants, children and adult, shoes, every sort of cosmetic, scarves, and bed sheets.

The price offered range greatly; there are some cheap ones but there are also expensive products, the latter on sale for high prices, sometimes reasonable. However, you still have to haggle to the best of your ability.

In one's spare time, individual travel is really good fun. There are places close to home, like Luxun Park. People can exercise and run in the fresh air. The park also offers a place for all types of activities like singing, dancing, instrumental performances, badminton, boating and even gambling. Every day from morning until afternoon, the park is very busy with people, particularly at the weekends. There are bigger parks in Shanghai, such as Zhongshan Park and Century Park but these are a bit far from where I live.

The top ports of call for visitors from all over the world when they come to Shanghai are the Oriental Pearl TV Tower, the Shanghai Science & Technology Museum, and the China Art Palace. The Oriental Pearl is one of the city's landmarks. People don't feel like they've seen the city unless they visit it. The 468m-high TV broadcast tower has become a venue for receiving VIPs. The tower is divided into many floors, one of which is the revolving restaurant with views of the city. Beside the tower flows the Huangpu River, full of boats. The view from the tower at night is beautiful; the lights give a wonderful sparkle to the scene.

Not far from the tower is the Shanghai Museum. Inside is an extensive collection of ancient artefacts from China's past. There are several special exhibits: bronze ware, ceramics, paintings, calligraphy, sculptures, jade, money, furniture, jade seals and local crafts.

A little further away from these two places is another museum, the China Art Museum. The building itself is very imposing; it is typically Chinese, red, and there are many stairs inside. The structure is supported by six large pillars that run up through the building. The museum houses many pieces of art, particularly those related to the film industry, with everything from the highly traditional to the modern.

Those with time on their hands can take a trip to Suzhou, which isn't far from Shanghai. There are a few sights there like the Yunyan Pagoda ("Leaning Tower of China"), Suzhou Museum and Lake Tai. The latter is really interesting. The lake is so wide that it's almost like the sea. In the middle of the lake are some huge pagodas that visitors can take a boat out to. The pagodas are home to an immense statue of Buddha, and offer beautiful views. In addition, there is a golden statue on the bank and a wall decorated with statues.

Apart from Suzhou, there's Hangzhou — the capital of Zhejiang Province and a bit further away from Shanghai. Still, it's only a 40-minute fast train ride away. The really well-known sight at Hangzhou is West Lake. The lake is very broad and almost surrounds the city. Around the lake are some beautiful buildings, as well as pagodas. Other than West Lake, there is a forest with a profusion of different plants, and with many different coloured leaves: green, yellow and red. It's a really relaxing atmosphere where you can learn about all kinds of plants.

Apart from shopping and travel, it's really interesting to go on a food tour. This is a natural addition to the other two past-times. There are all kinds of foods to prepare: breakfast, lunch or dinner. For breakfast there's tofu in brownish soup, with mushrooms, prawns, soybeans, coriander and hot peppers. Other than tofu, there are wontons, pork buns, or there's a sort of food made of white and black glutinous rice with all kinds of fillings like egg, meat, or sausage; or long sushi rolls. These are really good value for money — you can eat your fill for just 4-10 yuan. For lunch and dinner there are all kinds of cuisine on offer. Peking roast duck is really popular; the meat is prepared according to a traditional method that renders it really crispy and without a hint of the raw flavour. It's delicious. Other than duck, there is a lot of choice in terms of food — a plethora of fish, vegetables and mushrooms. Don't be surprised when the servings turn out to be huge. For me, the amounts given are too much for two people, let alone one.

There are many more interesting things I could say about Shanghai, despite a few less pleasant issues. The city government is doing its best to improve Shanghai as much as possible. One of the ways that is evident is the cleaners who work on station platforms, in shopping malls and restaurants. However, I could occasionally see people litter in the streets, which has somehow spoilt the beauty and cleanness of the city. Nonetheless, Shanghai is still fascinating for me. At some point in the future, I will definitely return. I love Shanghai.

About the author:

Eni Karlieni (Indonesian) graduated with a doctorate in linguistics from Padjadjaran University, where she teaches currently. Karlieni taught Indonesian at SISU's School of Asian and African Studies for two semesters in 2011 and 2014 respectively as part of the Partner University arrangement between Padjadjaran and SISU.

我眼中的上海

Eni Karlieni（印度尼西亚）

上海位于中国东海之滨的长江入海口，是中国历史文化名城之一。上海还是中国最大的工业城市和外贸港口城市。作为一个大都市，上海无论是在基础设施还是在市政建设方面都飞速发展：高层公寓巍然高耸，高架矗立，交通便利，似迷宫般的隧道迂回于地底，到处都有热闹的购物中心———一切安排都是为了满足社会的需要。

上海居民通常住在公寓里。这个5800平方公里的城市承载了两千五百万的居民，人口猛增使这座城市难以得到均衡发展。越来越多的公寓拔地而起，从朴素的到现代的，从便宜的到奢华的，上述不同公寓的风格和价格都与其中的各种设施相匹配。

地铁是这个城市中最广泛使用的公共交通工具。除了地铁，人们也使用公交车作为出行工具。地铁可以去往各个方向，几乎可以到达所有的地方，而且价格适当，速度相对较快。然而，在特定的时间，尤其是上下班时间，就不要指望可以在地铁中找到座位，因为那个时候地铁里挤满了乘客。尽管如此，与私家车相比，地铁仍然是一个更好的出行选择，因为不用担心堵车。

公路基础设施支撑着交通运输业的发展。五层甚至更多层的立交桥横亘在空中，通往各个方向。公路建设不仅往上发展，也穿透地面向下发展。像立交桥一样，地下道路也不止向下一层，而是很多层。真的很了不起啊！

上海的旅游景点各种各样，有包含地下层的大型购物中心，有市区和郊区的风景点，有传统和现代不同风格、价位不一的美食。所有这些的发展都与社会的发展相适应。

在南京路和淮海路有面向高端客户的购物中心，云集了各种知名品牌：路易威登、卡地亚、爱马仕、爱格纳、蔻依、蔻驰。然而，如果钱包不鼓，就不要尝试走进这些商店，因为里面价格很高。成千上万的人走过，或是购物，或是仅看看衣服、包、鞋、电子产品等。南京路上装饰着写有汉字的红灯笼。圣诞节前的街道和商店遍布喜庆的圣诞饰品。

至于我们这样的中低收入阶层，可以去一些大商场，比如说虹口龙之梦和人民广场、中山公园的一些购物中心，但更有趣的是去豫园、上海科技馆和七浦路。

豫园是一个引人入胜的地方。矗立的高墙，围绕着传统中国风格的建筑和一座被称为"玉园"的古老公园。它的建筑风格与传统的远东风格有细微差别，向上翘起的屋顶形成尖角，主色是红金色。这个公园是明代（1368–1644）遗迹。在豫园附近有各种购物中心，我们可以找到各种各样的玉石或宝石，作为具有中国风味的纪念品。商品一物一价，取决于顾客想要多好的质量；定价灵活，有可以还价的，也有不可以还价的。

如果你要买衣服、包、鞋、纪念品、围巾、针织桌布、珍珠等，可以去上海科技馆。这个地方不太热闹，气氛舒适。来这里的大多是外国人。卖家出的价是非常高的。我们必须善于讨价还价，要还到一半的价格。还价要有独特的方法：不要急于还价，直接走开直到商家叫我们回去；如果商家不叫我们回去的话，说明刚刚的价格就是低价。

七浦路是一个淘便宜货的地方。这是一个非常热闹的购物场所，吸引了大量顾客；七浦路还是批发贸易中心，以至于来这里的大多是商人。这里有各种各样的商品，比如：包，婴儿、青少年和成年人的衣服，鞋，各种化妆品，围巾，床单。卖家开出的价格不一，有卖低价的，也有卖高价的，但后者有时会以合理价格促销。然而，我们还是要尽量讨价还价。

有空闲时间时，自行出游是最让人开心的，我可以去离住处最近的地方——鲁迅公园。在这里，人们可以锻炼、呼吸着新鲜空气跑步，也可以进行各种各样的活动，比如唱歌、跳舞、演奏乐器、打羽毛球、划船，这里甚至有赌博的。每天从早上到下午，这里都很热闹，特别是在周末的时候。除了鲁迅公园，上海还有更大的公园，比如中山公园和世纪公园。然而，那些公园离我住的地方稍微有点远。

来上海旅游的各国游客首选的旅游目的地有东方明珠塔、上海博物馆和中华艺术宫。东方明珠塔是上海的城市标志。如果没去东方明珠塔，人们会感觉没去过上海。这座高达468米的塔提供广播电视信号，也成为接待重要客人的地方。东方明珠塔里面有很多层，其中一层是可以看到上海市景的旋转餐厅。在东方明珠塔周围就是黄浦江，江中有很多船只，晚上的景色非常美丽，灯饰让两岸的夜景显得十分璀璨。

离东方明珠塔不远就是上海博物馆。这个博物馆里面收藏着各种各样的中国历史文物。专题馆包括：青铜馆、陶瓷馆、绘画馆、书法馆、雕塑馆、玉器馆、钱币馆、家具馆、玺印馆和民族工艺馆。

除此之外，离这两处有点远的地方有另一个博物馆，即中华艺术宫。这个建筑看起来非常雄伟壮观，极富中国特色，通体红色，内部有很多阶梯。它由底部六根垂直向上的大柱子支撑。中华艺术宫展出从传统到现代的各类艺术品，尤其是与电影业有关的。

如果你有空闲时间的话，你可以去离上海不远的苏州。那儿的景点有虎丘云岩寺塔（被称为"中国斜塔"）、苏州博物馆以及太湖。太湖非常有趣，湖面宽广，几乎和海差不多。在湖的中间有一些非常大的塔。我们可以乘船去塔那边。塔里有非常大的佛像，从塔上我们可以眺望美丽的风景。除此之外，在岸边有一尊金色的佛像和装饰着小雕像的墙壁。

除了苏州，我们也可以去浙江省的省会——杭州。杭州离上海有些远。但是，坐动车40分钟就可以到了。杭州的一大著名景点是西湖。西湖非常宽广，几乎围绕了整座城。在湖的四周有一些非常好看的屋舍和塔。除了西湖，杭州还有森林可供游玩，森林里有各种植物，长着缤纷多彩的叶子，有绿色、黄色、红色。这里的氛围非常舒适，我们可以学习认识各种各样的植物。

除了购物和旅行，另一件十分有趣也是必做不可的事就是尝遍美食。早、中、晚三顿饭都有琳琅满目的美食可供选择。早饭我们可以享受拌着酱汁的豆腐，里面有菌菇、小虾、豆子、香菜和辣椒。除了豆腐，还有馄饨、肉包子，以及一种由黑白糯米制成的长条饭卷，里面包着鸡蛋、肉、香肠等馅料。这些食物的价格非常实惠，只要4到10块钱就可以吃饱了。中饭和晚饭，我们可以尝试不同的菜单。北京烤鸭是很受欢迎的佳肴，用非常传统的方法烹饪，以至于鸭肉尝起来非常松脆，没有腥气，十分美味。除了鸭，还有很多种可供选择的食物，比如各种鱼、蔬菜、菌菇。你不要惊讶，这些菜端上来的分量都非常多。对我来说，不要说是自己吃，就算是两个人吃，这个分量也还是太多了。

还有很多关于上海的趣事可以说，不过，我多少也会遇到一些我不太看得惯的地方。上海市政府努力将这个城市建设得尽可能的好。其中之一就是在站台、商场、餐厅等地配备清洁工。但是，我还是观察到有一些人在街上乱丢垃圾，影响了环境的整洁美观。尽管如此，我眼中的上海丝毫不减其绚丽多姿。在未来的某个时候，我一定还会回来。我爱上海。

作者简介：

Eni Karlieni（印度尼西亚籍）毕业于印尼巴查查兰大学语言学博士学位，现担任印尼巴查查兰大学教师，分别于2011年和2014年被派往上海外国语大学东方语学院担任印尼语专业教师。

A BEIJING STORY

Ourania Katavouta

I write my Beijing story so as to help my memory when I am old, to transform into words all those pretty images I saw and experienced in the North Capital (Beijing) of so many Chinese dynasties. I write and I listen to buddhist mantra from a CD I bought outside Lama Temple at Yonghegong Dajie. I returned sick but so full of emotions about my visit to this city. So, I am thinking "I want more Beijing!"

What can I say about Beijing… It's so huge and… imperial! First time there, getting out of metro and trying to find my hotel. Qianmen station, just below Tian'anmen Square. There was sunshine and a clear blue sky, and I saw one of these big gates that used to lead to the Forbidden City in the past. As usual, I made some circles until I found my hotel, hidden in a hutong, these old narrow streets of the city. My hotel was built in a courtyard, really lovely. A laughing Buddha welcomed me — first thing I met while going towards my room. There were many colors and lanterns in the internal balconies. Every morning, the hotel smelt sandalwood from the burned joss sticks in front of the Buddha.

Running to the Temple of Heaven

It was cold in Beijing, really cold even if it was only November. The first thing I bought was a warm cap (nowhere without it for the next days and nights). I ran to the first sight, the Temple of Heaven. Well, this was one of the most beautiful parks I had ever seen in China and one of the largest. It was sunset time, the colors in the sky and in the park were really beautiful, with autumn yellow leaves, a sharp wind and the Temple. It was the most beautiful temple of all I had seen, the imperial blue and yellow were unique here. I took pictures, I sat on a bench, really freezing. I watched older people playing cards or Chinese chess, and I was only a few hours in Beijing, frozen but so glad! I went back to Qianmen, just hanging around in the street and realizing that there was a full moon! So, first day in Beijing perfectly ended!

No kites at Tian'anmen

The biggest square in the world — 40,000 square meters. It is a monument for the people of China, a significant historic centre and now the most well-guarded area in Beijing. If I had to write an essay like these ones in primary school about the subject "I think and I write: What I saw at Tian'anmen", I would write about the old men, the grandparents I saw there, with their woolen coats, their faces burned by the sun and the wind, about these who came at the big square to see Mao Zedong. I would write about these people who visit Tian'anmen not only as tourists or wanderers but because they feel like visiting the most important square of their country. And it's true. It is the most important. I only feel sorry that kites are not allowed in Tian'anmen like in other squares or parks in China. These red birds made of paper would perfectly fit in there. And, basically, flying kites is something that usually older people do. So, I dedicate this text to Chinese grandparents and the missing kites over Tian'anmen.

A walking story

They say that once you start walking in Beijing, you forget to stop. And this is true. It is huge, it is flat and full of sights. Was I an Alice in Wonderland? Was I more a tourist or an old time's wanderer? What was this that made you walk an hour just to find an interesting place to eat something unique in this Beijing? Was it curiosity? Or was it just the nature of this person that was born to walk?

The following days in Beijing included all the classic visits to the Forbidden City, the Jingshan Park, the Summer Palace, many temples, the beautiful Beihai Lake and the lifetime experience in the Great Wall. Last day, I decided to visit Chairman Mao's Memorial Hall. I felt really strange, for I knew that this was a very unique moment. I couldn't explain the feeling. Lastly, I visited the enormous National Museum and, of course, I couldn't see many things but I was lucky! There was an exhibition about Leo Tolstoy, so I went there to see the manuscripts of *Anna Karenina* and I finished my visit with the recent history of China. I had to hurry, because it was crowded in the metro and I had a train to catch up! I came back to Shanghai exhausted and sick but totally satisfied.

To sum up, thinking back my trip, I consider Beijing more "original" China. But I prefer to live in Shanghai. I have the impression that Shanghai is more "western friendly", even if I don't have any specific reason about it. Maybe because there are more foreigners here and the social environment is more western. Or maybe it is just my sense. Besides, Shanghai is my home right now!

About the author:

Ourania Katavouta (Greek) graduated with a master's degree in Modern Linguistics from Aristotle University of Thessaloniki, Greece before teaching Greek at the Department of Western Languages, SISU.

北京故事

Ourania Katavouta（希腊）

我记录下我的北京故事，以后当我老了，就可以将这些文字化作美好的画面，回忆起我在北京这个中国北方历朝古都的所见所闻。我边听着我从雍和宫大街的喇嘛寺庙外买回的梵乐CD，一边写下这段文字。从北京回来后我病了，但是我心中却充满了对这座城市的感情。我想，"北京我还看不够！"

对于北京，该从何说起呢？它是那么大，那么充满皇家气概！我从地铁下来，试图找到我预订的酒店。那是前门站，就在天安门广场底下。那天阳光明媚，天空碧蓝如洗，我看到了那些历史上通往紫禁城的巨大城门。和往常一样，我绕了几个圈才找到酒店，它隐藏在胡同深处，这些胡同古老逼仄。酒店在一个庭院里，非常有格调。在去房间的路上，一个笑面佛在欢迎我。房间的阳台色彩艳丽，挂着灯笼。每天清晨，我都能闻到笑面佛前燃香所散发出的类似檀香木一样的香味。

奔向天坛

尽管才11月，北京就已经非常冷了。我买了一顶暖和的帽子，结果接下来的日子里不管是白天还是晚上都离不开它。我参观的第一个景点是天坛公园。这是我在中国去过的最大最美的公园之一。日暮时分，天空和公园交相辉映。金黄色的落叶、凌厉的冷风以及宫殿，这里是我见过的最美丽的庙宇了，庄严的蓝色和黄色互相映衬，十分特别。我拍了照片，坐在一个石凳上，被冻僵了。周围有很多老人在打牌或者下象棋。我来到北京仅仅几个小时，尽管被冻僵了，但是心里很高兴。我回到前门，在街上闲逛，竟然看到天上的满月。第一天的北京之行就这样完美落幕了！

天安门没有风筝

天安门面积达4万多平方米，是世界上最大的广场。这里对中国人民具有重大象征意义，它是历史的中心，现在是北京安保最严的地方。如果我是小学生，要写一篇《所思所想——我看到的天安门》，我会写这里的老人，穿着棉衣的爷爷奶奶，他们的面庞被烈日和寒风侵蚀了，但是他们专程过来看毛泽东。我还会写游览天安门广场的人，他们不仅仅是游客或者闲逛的人，他们来是想亲眼目睹这个国家最重要的广场。这是真的，这里的确是最重要的地方。

我只是为没能看见广场上空飘扬的风筝而感到遗憾。中国的其他公园或者广场是允许放风筝的。那些红色的大鸟风筝对于天安门广场来说是再合适不过了，一般只有老年人才放风筝，所以我将此文献给那些中国的老人以及天安门广场天空中缺席的风筝。

在北京散步

人们说，一旦你在北京散步，你就会忘记停下来。这是真的。北京太大了，一马平川，到处都是景点。我是不是像爱丽丝漫游到了仙境？我是一个游客还是一个旧时光的漫游者？是什么能让人走整整一小时去找寻一家北京的特色小吃店？是好奇心吗？抑或是人类与生俱来的走路本能？

在接下来的几天里，我去了北京的经典旅游景点：紫禁城、景山公园、颐和园、数不胜数的庙宇、美丽的北海以及长城——登长城堪称终生难忘的经历。最后一天，我决定去参观毛主席纪念堂。在那里，我感觉很奇妙，我知道这是一个特殊的时刻。我很难解释内心的感受。最后，我去了巨大的中国国家博物馆，当然了，我没法看完所有的展品，但是我很幸运，那天刚好有托尔斯泰展览，所以我看到了《安娜·卡列尼娜》的手写稿。最后，我观看了近代中国史的展览。我必须赶路，地铁里很拥挤，但我要去赶火车。回到上海后，我筋疲力尽，还病了一场，但是满心欢喜。

对于我的北京之行，我想说，北京是更"原汁原味"的中国。但是我更喜欢住在上海。我的感觉是上海对西方人更友好，尽管我解释不了为什么。也许是因为这里有更多的外国人，社会环境也更加国际化。也许这仅仅是我的感觉。不管怎么说，现在上海才是我的家。

作者简介：

Ourania Katavouta（希腊籍）毕业于塞萨洛尼基亚里士多德大学现代希腊语言学硕士学位，现担任上海外国语大学西方语学院希腊语专业教师。

LOVE IN SHANGHAI

Paul Robert Hofman

I always ask the boys why they carry their girlfriend's handbag. On the metro, at University, in the shopping malls — you see the boys clutching these bags as if they were worth more than life itself.

The girls walk confidently, unencumbered by any belongings, often clutching their boyfriend as if they were still connected to the bag but through another medium. The couples — glamorous and carefree — shop, smile and revel in their freedom to make their own choices and express themselves.

Of course, it is a signal of ownership, commitment and status. Both have found someone who is willing to make a public show of their togetherness.

I ask the boys whether they feel awkward or embarrassed carrying around a handbag but no one so far has admitted any such feelings. The men of Shanghai, famous for their tenderness towards their women, see this as another way to show their commitment to the girl. In Sydney on the other hand, carrying around one's girlfriend's bag would be considered emasculating and perhaps demeaning for the man. For the women, giving up their bag would be thought of as giving up their independence and they would be suspicious of any men who would like to carry their bag.

Shanghainese girls have no issues with this practice; it seems normal for the man to carry their bag as a sign that they are together. It's as if a ring is not big enough and the bag is a more potent signal.

In this time of increasing wealth, material values and social change, in a way, carrying the bag connects everyone to another time where little gestures took on meaning when possessions were less important. Suddenly, the bag has taken on greater significance and almost become a gateway to another era. Simplicity, stability and certainty.

The couples probably do not realise it but this act connects them with their parents and grandparents in a profound way. Shanghai is a world-famous mega city but it is made up of people continuing the rhythms of relationships that resonate with everyone.

Who would have thought it: Gucci, LV and Prada — a simple gesture, not of wealth, but of love.

About the author:

Paul Robert Hofman (Australian) graduated with a master's degree in economics and industrial relations at UNSW, and currently teaches at SISU Overseas Training Centre.

上海的爱情

Paul Robert Hofman（澳大利亚）

我经常问一些男孩：为什么要帮自己的女朋友拎包？在地铁上，大学校园中，商场里……随处可见将女朋友的包紧紧拽在自己手里的男孩子——好像包比他们的生命还要重要。

而男孩身边的女孩子手中却空无一物，她们自信满满，紧紧挽着身边的男友，似乎通过男友这个媒介她们仍然得以控制自己的手提包。一对对情侣们光鲜亮丽、无忧无虑、笑容满面，尽情沉浸在自由选择和表达自我的快乐中。

当然，这种行为体现了占有、承诺和地位。两个人都乐意通过这种公开行为向外界宣告：我们在一起。

我问男孩子们是否觉得帮女友拎包尴尬或别扭，至今为止，还没有哪个男孩承认有这样的感受。上海男人素以体贴和照顾女性闻名，他们将拎包的行为看成是表达自己爱意的方式。相反，在悉尼，帮女人拎包的男人会被认为缺乏男子气概，甚至有损人格；对女性来讲，把自己的手提包给男人会被视作放弃她们的独立，而她们对主动帮自己拎包的男人也会有所疑虑。

但上海女孩子完全没有这样的顾虑，让男人帮自己拎包是再正常不过的事了，这表明两个人在一起的亲密关系，就好像戒指太小还不够醒目，不如拎包这个行为来得更加明显。

在这个财富日益增长、以物质来衡量价值、社会不断变化的时代，男性帮女性拎包这一行为使人联想到过去，那时，一个小小的举动都富含意味，物质还不那么重要。突然之间，拎包所体现出的重要意义几乎让我们窥见过去的时代：简单、稳固和坚定。

也许情侣们并没有意识到，但这一行为却将他们和他们的父辈、祖辈深深联系在了一起。上海是举世闻名的国际都市，但是这里的人们却传承着爱情的古今韵律。

谁会想到呢，古驰、路易·威登和普拉达——象征的不是财富，而是爱情。

作者简介：

Paul Robert Hofman（澳大利亚籍）毕业于新南威尔士大学经济及工业关系硕士学位，现担任上海外国语大学出国培训部教师。

MAKING SENSE OF CHINA

Romain Vuattoux

For many foreigners, China is a mystical faraway land with a strange difficult language, an ancient complex culture and an unexplainable economic miracle, sometimes praised and sometimes demonized by Western media. Much of these perceptions are stereotyped and biased, and it is not until these foreigners come to China that their mind begins to change and their preconceived ideas shatter to pieces. Yet more confusion and strong feelings, such as surprise, frustration and loneliness, usually arise from the experience of living in China. One can only wonder: How can such a foreign place feel so much like home yet be so different? How can such a place generate so many contradictory feelings? Why is all of this so confusing?

My relationship with China dates back to a short summer exchange program in 2003. I have had many contradictory experiences in China, and find it difficult to come up with the words that capture my feelings and enable me to express one story about China. Rather than a specific description of a particular event, moment, or story, my story about China is more a collection of stories and anecdotes, which form my memory and capture my feelings about China.

One anecdote illustrates the way I have been treated in China. When I came to live in China in early 2007, I resided in a "small town" of 300,000 people — in fact the largest city I had ever lived in. My colleague and I were the only two foreigners in town, and we were treated with the traditional hospitality given to "faraway guests". A committee had been arranged to welcome us to the school, signs had been hung over the gate of the school welcoming us in large characters, and flowers were handed to us as we got out of the car. All of this was overwhelming, but a clear illustration of the hospitality I would receive for the following four years, until I moved to Shanghai, where I became "just another foreigner". On that first day, we were invited to a formal welcome dinner. We were picked up and driven to a very fancy and luxurious restaurant. When we were offered drinks, to our great surprise, the waiter offered to warm the beer in a kettle. That was the first tilt in the evening, for something strange was occurring: what we were used to (i.e. beer is drunk cold) was in fact abnormal to our host (in that town beer was warmed up in the winter). As the evening moved on, and as the "ganbei" (bottoms up) became more intense, our hosts relaxed, the language barrier seemed to dissipate and the previous formal ceremonial atmosphere dropped. I would later find out that in many ways similar to France, the importance of the bounds created during meals and these drinking sessions became an essential part of celebration and connections. It was also the method that would enable me to begin reaching an understanding of China.

From the first day I arrived in China, it has been an *explosion of the senses*. The first sense that was stimulated was the sense of *smell*. China has a specific smell, which you recognize when you land at the airport (especially in the summer) and when you walk on the streets. In the warm humid summer air of southern cities such as Shanghai, it is a mixture of food, sweat, pollution, exhausts, garbage and sewer. Most probably the preeminent fragrances a foreigner associates with China is that of street food and especially the odor of "choudoufu" (stinky tofu) and that of "baijiu" (rice wine). Every foreigner who has lived in China remembers the first time they wondered what animal had died nearby, and many have great tales of their first trial at eating "choudoufu", or drinking "baijiu".

Hearing is probably the sense that is excited in the most unpleasant manner. From people yelling on the phone in a congested metro or bus, to the constant honking of motorbikes, e-bikes, cars and even bicycles, or the bells of street sellers and collectors, the noises made by construction sites, the ears are never left alone and silence is often hard to find. Even in parks, hordes of tourists follow guides on megaphones, and old people sing at full blast on improvised KTV. My personal funniest story about sounds was the first morning I woke up in China. It was early in the morning, I was jetlagged and a rooster was singing to the rising sun. After getting up, I investigated the origin of the sound. The rooster was not outside, but inside the echoing staircase, tied by the leg to the handrail of the building. As I inquired about the disappearance of the rooster a few days later (which pleased me as I could finally sleep), I learnt that this loud creature was in fact the dinner of my upstairs neighbors. Fresh as it comes!

Our sense of *sight* is aroused daily. Walking or cycling on the streets requires paying attention to all the obstacles on the sidewalks or on the roads at all time. A small moment of carelessness, especially during rush-hour, you can easily find yourself running into another cyclist, or worse a pedestrian. Yet, the biggest "visual attack" is probably the urban development going on around at all time and at indefinable speed. I have seen cities changing, disappearing or being built at amazing speed where there were only rice paddies and vegetables. Beyond the architectural feats, I have seen some of the most modern and advanced technology in Shanghai, and travelled back in time in underdeveloped, remote villages in the mountains, where people live a simple and quiet life, far from the speed and stress of the cities and far from all the advanced technologies, almost as if they were stuck in another time. I have seen the beauty of natural sceneries in the countryside. I have seen the fast movement of commuters amidst the immobility of old people sitting in the sun on the sidewalk, or the slow motion of "taichi" disciples in the park among the square-dancing women. I have seen the contrast between the heteroclite hairstyles and fashionable clothes of the youth and the old-fashioned outfits of the seniors. Similarly to the contrast observed between old decrepit buildings and modern towers, poor neighborhoods and wealthy gated communities, or the impeccable cleanliness of government buildings, adjacent to landfills. Even once my eyes are closed, I often dream of these sights.

The sense of *touch* is best illustrated by two experiences I had when I first came to China. I call these "being an unknown super star" and "being touched". In my first educational establishment, I sometimes had to teach in another campus on the other side of town. I would ride my bicycle across town to get to class, and it often felt like being in a movie. All the kids and many of the adults stared and pointed to the "laowai" (foreigner) or "meiguoren" (American) on his bicycle. I am not sure if I felt I was Godzilla strolling through town or Michael Jackson walking on the street, causing amazement and surprise. As I took excursions in the "deep" countryside, many people would approach me while I was buying some water or some snack and would start touching the hair on my arms.

The other experience of "being touched" was when I was sent to a partnership school in a remote location to give a short introduction about France to a few selected students from each class of the partner school. When I arrived on the campus, the whole school was waiting for me at the windows. Kids were hanging and shouting out of every barred window: "Laowai!" Shortly after my arrival, I was taken through the whole hierarchy of the school and invited to drink tea in every office, unconsciously ingurgitating large amounts of water in small doses. My introduction lasted about 45 minutes at which point I really needed to answer a "call of nature" (as is often posted in Chinese toilets). However, my students were determined to obtain an autograph on every book they had, and would not let me go until I signed every last book. After completing this task while being pushed around by students who were trying impatiently to climb on top of each other to get their book signed first, I finally managed to get out of the room. However, the other half of the school was waiting outside, and had the exact same request. At that point, I could no longer hold and so apologetically pushed my way to the men's room while promising I would return to fulfill everyone's demand after I had "taken care of business". As I entered my intended destination, mass hysteria continued and a dozen boy students made their way in the facility with me. The struggle continued until I could finally achieve my goal. I never imagined I would feel the pressure of being a "super star" in such a way, especially as I was just an ordinary foreigner. The lack of privacy and personal space can sometimes be bothersome in China. However, I could not help but notice the indifference and anonymity of walking on the street when I went back to Europe, where eye contact is usually avoided with any stranger in public spaces.

For foreigners as for Chinese, the most important sense is the sense of *taste*. It is also certainly the one that provides the most pleasure and the base of many relationships, from friends to colleagues. I have been invited to many meals and took part in ceremonial drinking as described above. I have also tasted foods I had never imagined I would eat or even knew existed. I have seen food displays that are as elaborate as their tastes. Thousand-year-old eggs, snake, turtle, "baozi" (steamed bun), dumplings, bamboo, lotus root, pigs ears, lacquered duck, duck neck and head, chicken feet, spicy fish head, the hundreds of ways of eating tofu are just some of the dishes that one discovers and appreciates. A lifetime would never suffice to try to taste all the specialties. The flavors are also incredible to explore, sour, sweet, spicy, salty, acid and combinations endless. If there is a place where it is possible to eat at any price and any time of the day, and a place to eat something different for every meal, China is the place.

Orderly chaos, disorganized order, old and new, beautiful and filthy, clean and dirty, rich and poor, kindness and arrogance... All are opposed sensations and situations living together, side by side. For me, China is a collision of feelings, a juxtaposition of experiences and perceptions that are usually contradictory. China is all these contradictions and diversity that somehow manage to live together almost harmoniously. I have developed friendships with the most improbable people imaginable, from entrepreneurs, CEOs, politicians, to farmers, unemployed, retired people, shopkeepers or hairdressers. I have been welcomed and treated as a special honorable guest, with great respect, even though I had done nothing particular to deserve such treatment. Every thing was so foreign and strange to me, yet China has slowly become my home, and home has become foreign.

In France, life seems stuck in a moment, stagnating, unchanged, still. A friend of mine described this by saying: "China is a *developing* country. Europe is *developed*." As an English teacher, the tense emphasis does not go unnoticed, and it describes well how Europe has stopped looking forward, has stopped embracing diversity and change. What is most engaging and sometimes frustrating in China is the way people are unconditionally optimistic about the future, so ready to embrace change and at the same time, sometimes, so reluctant to do so. How the Chinese people are curious and open to new ideas while sometimes caught up in traditions! Maybe this is not all that different from Europe where differences also exist, but in China these oppositions are exacerbated by the size of the country and the speed of the development. As a foreigner they strike you even more, because they are foreign. To me, France is becoming increasingly stagnant, closed on itself, intolerant towards non-Europeans. As opposed to the predictable, sanitized, standardized comfort of France which tames my senses (I will admit an exception for cheese and wine), China awakens your senses and makes you feel alive, it forces you to have feelings. Chinese people have an attitude that makes everything seem possible, while the French are nowadays pessimistic and resigned. China is alive and France is asleep. For some foreigners this is just too much to take in, but for me this daily thrill keeps me awake and alive. For many foreigners their relationship with China is a love-hate relationship. For me it is the constant buzz, changes and contradictions described above that I miss when I am not in China. As I spend more time in China, I find myself gaining understanding and becoming more knowledgeable, yet growing increasingly confused and at ease with this confusion.

I have met foreigners in China who refused to open their senses, to taste Chinese food, to "feel China", to open their minds, and those foreigners often had a very bad time here. Someone once told me "China makes you or breaks you". While I think it is not completely wrong, I would rather argue that it pushes you out of your comfort zone and wakes you to your senses, it forces you to feel. Hopefully, my story can inspire others to open their senses to "make sense" of China, to feel and embrace life around them.

About the author:

Romain Jean-Marie Vuattoux (French) graduated with a Master's Degree from the University of Malmo, Sweden, and currently teaches at SISU Overseas Training Centre.

解读中国

Romain Vuattoux（法国）

对很多外国人来讲，中国是一个遥远而神秘的国度。那里的人讲着奇怪难懂的语言，有着古老深奥的文化和难以解释的经济奇迹，有时被西方媒体称赞，有时又被其妖魔化。这是大多数外国人对中国的固有印象，这种印象往往带有偏见。直到外国人亲自来到中国，他们的看法才会发生转变，他们对中国原有的主观想法会分崩离析。随着在中国生活的时日增多，他们会产生更多的困惑以及惊奇、挫败和孤独等其他强烈的感受。你不禁会问自己：为什么这样一个国家和自己的母国如此相似而又如此迥异？为什么这个国家给人如此矛盾的感觉？为什么这一切都让人如此不解？

我和中国的缘分始于2003年的短期暑期交流项目。从那以后，我在中国的体验是如此矛盾，以至于我很难用词语去形容，也很难用区区一个故事来描述。与其描述某个特定的事件、时刻或故事，还不如我讲几个小故事，它们存在于我的记忆中，折射出我对中国的感受。

第一个故事是关于我是如何被中国人对待的。2007年初，我来到中国生活。当时我住在一个有30万人口的"小"城镇——事实上，这是我从小到大住过的人口最多的地方。我和我的同事是这个镇上仅有的两个外国人，于是，我们受到了当地人对待"远道而来的客人"的盛情款待。他们安排了专门的人员队伍将我们接到学校，校门口挂着写有大字的横幅，欢迎我们的到来。我们下车时收到了他们献上的鲜花。这般礼遇让我们受宠若惊。在此后四年间，我们一直都受到这样的热情款待——这一情况直到我后来搬到上海才发生了改变，因为在上海，我只是不起眼的"普通外国人"。话说回来，在我们抵达小镇的当天，人们邀请我们去参加正式的欢迎宴会。我们被接到一个非常豪华奢侈的酒店。当服务员端上饮料时，他竟然提出可以帮我们把啤酒倒进开水壶热一热，这让我们颇为惊异。这是当晚的第一个小插曲。我们自认为正确的道理（比如啤酒应该是冰镇着喝的）在我们的主人看来却很奇怪（当地人冬天喝啤酒前都要热一下）。在接下来的时间里，随着"干杯"的次数越来越多，我们的主人逐渐放松了，语言障碍似乎在消失，之前的拘束礼节也放下了。后来，我发现这一点和法国很相似，比如在庆祝活动或者人际交往中，很多重要的纽带都是通过饭桌和喝酒培养的。这也成为我后来开始接触和理解中国人的一种方式。

自打第一天到达中国，我就陷入了各种"感官轰炸"。第一个被激发的感觉是"嗅觉"。中国有种独一无二的气味，这种气味从你一到机场、走在街上就能辨别出来（尤其在夏天）。在南方城市比如上海，夏季空气往往湿热，这种气味融合了食物、汗液、污染、废气、垃圾以及发酵物所散发出的种种味道。对于一个外国人来说，这种特有的混合气味中，首当其冲的可能是地摊小吃的味道，尤其是诸如臭豆腐或者白酒这样的味道。每一个住在中国的外国人都记得他们初来时会时常纳闷是不是周边有腐烂的动物尸体，很多外国人也都对他们第一次吃臭豆腐或者喝白酒的经历津津乐道。

"听觉"无疑是被触发的最不愉快的一种感受。在拥挤的地铁或公交车上对着手机大喊大叫的人，摩托车、电瓶车、小轿车甚至是自行车所发出的令人厌烦的揿铃和喇叭声，街头小贩和收垃圾者的吆喝声，建筑工地的噪声……各种声音夹杂在一起，让耳朵没有片刻的宁静。即便在公园也是如此：带着一群游客的导游用扩音器讲解，老人们举着简易麦克风用最大的音量吊嗓子。我自己经历过的最有趣的事情发生于我在上海醒来的第一个早晨。那时候还很早，我仍在倒时差。忽然，我听到伴随着太阳升起的鸡鸣声。起床后，我去追踪这一声音的来源。原来那只公鸡并不在室外，而是一只脚被拴在极具回音效果的楼道里。几天后，这只公鸡消失了，这让我暗自窃喜，因为我终于可以睡个安稳觉了。当问起其下落时，我被告知这个叫声嘹亮的生物已经成了我楼上邻居的盘中餐。多么新鲜的食材！

我们的"视觉"每天都在被唤醒。当你在路上行走或者骑车时，你必须对人行道或者马路上的任何障碍物都时刻保持警惕。尤其在交通高峰，一不留神就可能与其他车辆甚至行人发生"冲突"造成危险。然而，最大的视觉冲击是无时无刻不在进行中的市政工程建设。我看到了城市面貌的飞速变化，原先还是稻田或菜园的地方被改造重建，旧貌换新颜。除了这些建设成就，我还在上海看到了最新、最先进的科技；我去过一些欠发达地区和偏远的山村，那里的人们过着简单安逸的生活，远离城市的飞速发展和生活压力，远离所有的发达科技，他们就如同生活在一个不同的时空。我在乡下领略过大自然的美景；我看到在路边晒太阳的行动不便的老人和他们身边匆匆走过的上班族；我看到在公园中一招一式打太极拳的老者以及跳着欢快广场舞的大妈；我看到留着不规则发型、身着奇装异服的时髦青年和衣着保守的老年人。同样鲜明的对比也体现在老旧建筑与现代摩天大楼之间、破败街道与高档小区之间、崭新的政府大楼与其附近的垃圾填埋场之间。即使闭上眼，我依然会梦见这些场景。

关于"触觉"，我想用我初到中国时经历的两件趣事来诠释。我将这种体验称为"成为不知名的巨星"或者"被人触摸"。在我刚开始做教师时，我有时要去小镇另一头的校园上课。当我每次骑车穿过小镇去上课时，我经常觉得自己像是在拍电影。所有的小孩子和很多大人都会一边盯着我，一边对我指指点点，称我是"老外"或者"美国人"。我怀疑自己是否被视为横行在小镇中的哥斯拉，抑或是走在街上的迈克尔·杰克逊，不然怎会引来如此万众瞩目。有时我会深入乡间漫步，当我买水或者买吃的东西时，很多人都会靠近我，伸手触摸我胳膊上的汗毛。

另一个关于被"触摸"的经历发生在我被派往一个姐妹学校做介绍法国的小讲座过程中。那个学校地处偏远，我的听众是从各个班级挑选出来的学生。当我抵达学校的时候，所有的学生都趴在窗户旁等着看我。小孩子们从窗户的栏杆中探头出来，大喊"老外！"到达后不久，我就被引见给所有校领导，并且被每个办公室邀请喝茶，我不知不觉饮下了总量巨大的一杯杯茶。之后，当讲座进行到第45分钟时，我实在抑制不住去解手的生理需求。然而，学生们坚决不让我离开，他们争先恐后，巴不得我在他们所有能找到的书上签名。我一边完成了签名的任务，一边奋力挣脱蜂拥上前的学生，最后终于成功地逃出了教室。但教室外面还有更多的学生，他们同样要求我给每本书签名。这时，我已经走投无路，只好一边道歉并承诺"完事后"马上就给他们签名，一边奋力推开人群冲向男厕所。当我进到男厕所时，外面的狂热仍在继续，有几个男学生甚至跟着我冲进了厕所。这样的挣扎又持续了很久，直到我终于解决了内急。我从未想到自己会以这样的方式切身体会到作为明星的巨大压力，而我只是一个平凡的外国人。这种个人隐私和个人空间受到侵犯的感受的确令人困扰。与此同时，我不禁观察到在这一点上中国和欧洲的巨大差异，当你走在欧洲的街头，路人都是互不搭理、匆匆走过，在公共场合，陌生人之间都会小心避免眼神接触。

对外国人和中国人而言，"味觉"都是最重要的一种感官。它不仅给人提供了最多愉悦的享受，也促进人际关系的发展，如朋友之情和同事之情。如上文所说，我受邀出席过很多饭局和饮酒场合，我也尝试过很多曾经闻所未闻的食物，见过色香味俱全的菜式；像松花蛋、蛇肉、甲鱼、包子、饺子、竹笋、莲藕、猪耳朵、酱鸭、鸭脖子和鸭头、鸡爪、剁椒鱼头以及数百种吃豆腐的方式，只是我吃过的众多菜品中的一部分。至于所有的中国菜肴，恐怕一个人花一辈子的时间都无法尝遍。中国人饮食的口味也令人称奇：酸、甜、辣、咸等各种口味的组合无穷无尽。如果有一个地方能让人在任何时刻、以任何价位、每顿都吃不同的食物，那么，中国就是这个地方。

乱中有序、序中有乱、新旧相替、美好与丑陋、干净与肮脏、富有与贫穷、善良与傲慢……所有这些对立的感受和场景都并存在这个国度。对我来说，中国是一个能让外国人感官爆炸的国度，在这里各种令你措手不及的状况会让你充满矛盾的感觉。在中国，各种多元相悖的事物奇妙地和谐共处。我和一些最不可能成为朋友的中国人交上了朋友，从企业家、首席执行官、政治家到农民、失业者、退休老人、商贩或理发师。我受到很多人的欢迎，得到了贵宾般的礼遇，尽管我从未做过任何值得受到此般待遇的事情。虽然在中国经历的所有事情都如此新奇，但中国却在逐渐成为我的家，而我自己的母国却开始变得陌生。

在法国，生活似乎停滞在一个时刻，缺少变化，静止不动。我的一个朋友这样描述道："中国是一个正在发展的国家，而欧洲已经发展结束了。"作为一名英语教师，这句话的时态用法很难被忽视，它很好地表述了欧洲现在停滞不前的状态和缺乏拥抱多元文化、迎接变化的勇气。在中国，最吸引人、同时也让人时有挫败感的一点是，中国人对于未来无条件地乐观，他们非常乐意迎接变化，但同时又表现出内心的勉强。中国人是多么容易对新鲜事物感到好奇和包容，而同时又被拘泥于传统中啊！也许这和欧洲并非截然不同，但在中国，其广袤的国土面积和飞速的发展进一步加剧了这种矛盾的心理。作为一个外国人，我们受到的冲击更大，因为这一切都是陌生的。对我来说，法国正在日益变成一个停滞不前、自我封闭、对外来人愈加严苛的国家。法国可预见的、洁净的和标准化的舒适生活很容易麻痹人的感官（当然，我要承认奶酪和红酒是个例外），相反，中国却让你的感官觉醒，让你感到自己是活着的，它强迫你去感受。中国人有一种"万事皆有可能"的心态，而当今的法国人却变得日益悲观消极。中国是生机盎然的，而法国却在沉睡。对有些外国人来说，中国实在有点难以消化。但对我来说，每天的感官刺激让我能保持清醒和活力。对很多外国人来说，他们对中国的感情是爱恨交织。对我来说，它是连绵不断的喧闹、矛盾和变化，当我不在中国时，就会想念这一切。随着在中国生活的时间越来越长，我发现自己对中国的理解和认知也日渐加深，同样，我的困惑也越来越多，但我已经逐渐学会用处之泰然的心态面对它们。

在这里，我遇见了不少拒绝被中国影响的外国人，他们排斥中国的食物，拒绝"感受"中国，不愿敞开胸怀，而这些外国人往往有着非常糟糕的中国体验。有人曾经告诉我："中国要么成就你，要么打败你。"虽然我觉得这种说法有一定道理，但我更愿意表述为中国会促使你走出自己的"舒适区"，不断唤醒你的感官，强迫你去感受。我希望我的故事能够激励其他外国人，帮助他们打开自己的感官去理解中国，感受和拥抱中国的生活。

作者简介：

Romain Jean-Marie Vuattoux（法国籍）毕业于瑞典马尔默大学硕士学位，现担任上海外国语大学出国培训部教师。

二、体验篇

CHINESE BREAKFAST — BAOZI

Ben Keegan

My story concerns that most neglected of our three daily meals: breakfast. Given that it is the fuel that starts the engine of our bodies you'd think that greater attention would be paid to it. But both here in China and in my native Ireland, breakfast these days is often simply something to be shoveled into our mouths as quickly as possible before the working day begins. As a teacher with Shanghai International Studies University, my working day begins at 8 a.m. This is a full hour earlier than I was accustomed to back in Ireland, so breakfast has become even more of a perfunctory experience than it was at home. The story I'd like to share here concerns the breakfast I ate almost everyday for my first year in China, why I seldom eat it now and how I hope to one day soon be eating them every morning once again.

The first time I tried a "baozi", or a steamed bun, I instantly fell in love with it. Having found "zhou" (or rice gruel as we distastefully call it in English) inadequately interesting or substantial, the taste of steamed dough with a meat filling was far more Irish. The fact that these substantial hand-made treats were readily available on many street corners for what the English refer to as "tuppence" was a revelation to me. Each morning I would get one on the way to work from the inexplicably unpopular baozi stall next to my apartment. After chowing down on two of these each morning for six months, I decided that the meat filling of the "niurou" baozi was contributing to my expanding waistline. So I decided to switch to a vegetarian "cai" baozi. And much to the bemusement of the vendor, who was used to customers ordering two baozi at a time, I decided to eat only one. Having paid my 1 yuan (going vegetarian happily meaning that I could save 0.5 yuan per baozi, while quickly cutting a half kilo or "jin" off my waistline) I would cycle merrily to work, steering my bike with one hand and chomping on my breakfast with the other.

So why did I give up the joy of eating this most convenient, economical and hearty of breakfasts, you may now be asking yourself? Well, first off, I decided to move apartments and in my new abode there were no baozi stalls nearby and, to my horror, none on the route to work either. This meant that now the only stall I could frequent was the one next to my university building, which was completely overrun by students trying to grab their breakfast on the run. I discovered that while the queue these students formed in front of the baozi stall looked uniform enough, there were students keen to ignore the process of queuing and engage in the process of queue jumping. I, being from a monochronic culture where queues are seen as sacrosanct, had to decide on a daily basis between seeing people march to the front of the queue, or declare myself an unofficial policeman and alert them to the error of their ways. More often than not I found myself assuming the upright role of policeman, which may as well be an interesting and exotic intercultural experience when looking back.

So I went to Carrefour, bought a toaster and started eating toast with butter every morning just as I had in Ireland. At first the return of the comfort of a taste of home made me forget about the baozi stalls completely. But now I'm hankering to be able to enjoy the feel and taste of a piping hot baozi between my fingers and lips once again. So, I implore you. Next time you are at a baozi stall and you see people jumping the queue, please tell them of me and my desire to once again eat baozi for breakfast. But let them know that as long as they keep ignoring the vast majority of people queuing patiently in line, baozi will never taste as sweet as they could.

About the author:

Ben Keegan (Irish) graduated from Robert Gordon University, and currently teaches at SISU Overseas Training Centre.

中国的早餐——包子

Ben Keegan（爱尔兰）

　　我的故事是关于一日三餐中最容易被忽略的一餐——早餐。由于早餐是我们身体机能每日开始运转的燃料，你会认为早餐理应得到更多的重视。然而，在中国和我的祖国爱尔兰，早餐很容易沦为工作日开始之前胡乱塞进嘴里的东西。作为上海外国语大学的教师，我每天早上八点上班。这比我在爱尔兰所习惯的工作时间整整早一个小时。因此，我在这里的早餐比在爱尔兰更加敷衍了事。我在此想要跟大家一起分享我来中国后第一年每天早餐吃的是什么，为什么我现在几乎放弃了这种食物，以及我如何迫切希望能再次吃到这种食物。

当我第一次品尝"包子"（即一种蒸的点心）后，我立马就爱上了它。那时我觉得粥（在英文里，我们嫌弃地称之为大米稀饭）既无趣又缺乏实质内容，相比之下，蒸出来的肉包尝起来更加的"爱尔兰"。更何况这种耐吃的手工美味在很多街头巷尾都能找到，这让我实实在在体会到其价廉物美的好处。在每天早上去学校的路上，我都会在我家旁边的一个包子铺买包子吃。这个包子铺生意并不火，着实令我感到费解。在连续六个月每天早晨都吞下两个肉包子后，我开始意识到，这种牛肉包已然成为我腰身日渐凸显的原因之一。于是，我决定将牛肉包改成素菜包，而且每次只买一个，这让已经习惯卖给顾客两个包子的小贩觉得很困惑。在付好一块钱后（改吃菜包的另一个好处是每个包子可以省去5角钱，同时又可让我的体重在短时间内减轻一斤），我就边吃包子边骑自行车快快乐乐地去上班了。

那么，你可能要问，为什么我后来竟然放弃了吃这既方便又实惠的美味早餐的乐趣呢？首先，在我搬家之后，我的新住所周边竟然找不到类似的包子铺。更可怕的是，在我从新家到学校的途中竟然也没有包子铺！这意味着我不得不光顾学校教学楼旁边的那家包子铺，而那里永远挤满了早上急着去上课的学生顾客。这还不是最糟糕的，我很快发现，虽然在包子铺前等待的学生队伍看似整齐，但也时常会有不遵守规则的人插队。对于我这种来自于单一时间文化[1]背景的人来说，排队是神圣不可侵犯的。因此，我感觉自己

---

1 译者注："单一时间文化"也译为共时观念，在北欧和北美国家较为普遍。通常拥有这一时间概念的人惜时、重视时间，在同一时间内专心办妥一件事，不轻易分心，做事较有条理，不会随意改变计划，专注于完成当前的事。

每天都在做着两难的决定：要么眼睁睁地看着那些插队的人窜到队伍的最前面，要么我自己被迫成为业余警察，出面提醒或制止这种"不端行为"。多半情况下，我发现自己不自觉地承担了维护正义的业余警察角色，回头想想也算是一种异国的独特体验吧！

于是，我开始去家乐福买吐司，早上吃吐司蘸黄油的爱尔兰式早餐。起初，这回归了家乡口味的早餐让我完全忘记了曾经的包子。但现在，我又开始极度怀念起那热气腾腾的包子在指尖和唇齿间的感觉。我恳求你们，当你们以后买包子时，倘若看到插队者，请告诉他们我的故事，告诉他们我对早餐吃包子的渴求。同时，也请告诉他们，如果他们仍选择无视大多数耐心排队的人，包子将永远失去其应有的那般美味。

作者简介：

Ben Keegan（爱尔兰籍）毕业于罗伯特·戈登大学，现为上海外国语大学出国培训部教师。

ISRAEL AND CHINA

Miriam Beck-Freund

	Israel	China
Basic food	Pita/ bread/ halla	Rice
Drink	Nes coffee latte	Green tea
Tableware	Knife and fork	Chopsticks
Transportation	Private car/ bus/ train	Metro/ bus
Air	Fresh	Polluted
Sky	Blue	Grey
People	Various	Chinese
Population	7 million	1.5 billion
Pets	All kinds	Poodle
Public toilets	Very hard to find	Many in every corner
	Offer toilet paper/ soap	Offer nothing

Smoking in public	Prohibited	Everywhere
Offices	Personal decorations (paintings, posters)	No decorations at all
Children in family	3+	1+
Size	27,770 km^2	9.597 million km^2

I came from Israel, which is located in the Middle East, just the other side of Asia, and landed in the exotic China in the Far East, a year ago to be with my husband whom I missed very much. It is so good to live here in Shanghai not just as a tourist but for a longer stay, so I can explore the city.

I hung a map of Shanghai in my room and marked every Metro station that I visited with a yellow marker, and soon the whole map of Shanghai became yellow. I know every place, every Metro station — how it is from the inside to the outside.

I made not only Jewish friends from the communities but also some lovely good Chinese friends.

I really love to live in Shanghai, although it is not so easy at all. I learnt a little bit of Chinese in Mandarin House school and in WOW Mandarin school, and of course in SISU, but it is not enough. And the tones OMG! They are so difficult. I speak 5 languages but this is the hardest. Will I ever be understood in Chinese?

I like the Chinese food, whether sweet or sour, dry or watery; I like their textures and colors and above all their smells. I miss the real sweet cakes; here the cakes and bread are too soft.

The fruits are amazing! I have all the seasons at once, in the same time. Summer, autumn, winter, and spring, it doesn't matter. China is so huge, and the fruits of all seasons are here in the shops.

The other great thing here is of course TAOBAO, the ultimate shopping heaven! Things come straight to your doorstep.

Here was the first time that I did Chinese medicine treatment — a session of real acupuncture for losing weight. It really worked for me. Halleluiah! What fascinates me most is that the huge China is interested in the tiny Israel; it makes me very proud of my country — Israel.

About the author:

Miriam Beck-Freund (Israeli) graduated with a Master's Degree of Interdisciplinary Arts from Tel Aviv University and currently teaches Hebrew at the School of Oriental Languages, SISU.

以色列和中国

Miriam Beck-Freund（以色列）

	以色列	中国
食物	皮塔饼、面包、哈拉面包	米饭
饮料	咖啡拿铁	绿茶
餐具	刀叉	筷子
运输工具	私家车、公交车、火车	地铁、公交车
空气质量	清新	污染
天空	蓝色	灰色
人群构成	各族人	中国人
人口	700万	15亿
宠物	各种	贵宾犬
公厕	很难找到	几乎每个角落都有
	提供卫生纸/香皂	什么都没有
公共场所吸烟	禁止	到处都是
办公室	到处都是个人装饰品（画、海报）	什么都没有
孩子	3个以上	1个或2个
国土面积	20,770平方公里	959.7万平方公里

　　我来自以色列，它位于中东，坐落在亚洲的另一边。我在一年前来到了位于远东的异乡——中国，来和我思念已久的丈夫相聚。我很高兴自己是来上海久居而非旅游，因为这样我才能尽情探索这个城市。

　　我在自己房间的墙上挂了一张上海地图，把我去过的所有地铁站都用黄色荧光笔标记出来。没过多久，整张地图就变成了黄色。我去过每个地方，每个地铁站。

我在这里不仅交了很多犹太朋友，还交到很多可爱的中国朋友。

我非常喜欢住在上海，尽管这并不容易。我在一些培训机构学习了一点普通话，当然我在上海外国语大学也参加了中文课程班，但是这些还不够。汉语的音调实在是太难了，我能讲5种语言，但是汉语是最难的，不知道我说的中文有没有人能听懂。

我喜欢这里的食物，有酸有甜，有汤的有干的，食物的口感、颜色，尤其是味道都很棒。当然我也怀念家乡的甜蛋糕，这里的蛋糕和面包都太软了。

这里的水果太棒了！我随时都可以买到春夏秋冬各个季节的水果，也许是因为中国太大了，所以四季的水果都能供应。

另一个很棒的体验当然就是淘宝了，这真是购物的天堂，买好的东西可以直接被送到家门口。

我在这里第一次体验了中医真正的针灸疗法，这能帮助我减肥，而且作用显著！让我最着迷的是，这么大的中国会对小小的以色列感兴趣，这让我也为我的祖国感到自豪和骄傲。

作者简介：

Miriam Beck-Freund（以色列籍）毕业于特拉维夫大学跨学科艺术专业硕士学位，现担任上海外国语大学东方语学院希伯来语专业教师。

BECOMING A MOSLEM IN CHINA

Nani Darmayanti

Since March until July 2015, I have been assigned by Universitas Padjadjaran Bandung, my workplace, to teach Indonesian Language in the Indonesian Language Department, School of Asian and African Studies, Shanghai International Studies University (SISU). Even though it was the tenth year of this program (inviting lecturers of UNPAD to SISU), I was still worried when coming here. All along, it has been mostly men whom have been assigned. Meanwhile I am a woman wearing hijab. There were many questions before I came here. What was I supposed to eat? How was I supposed to practice my belief? How could I communicate? How could I socialize? And there were many questions on my mind. However, as an Indonesian, the philosophy of "*Di manabumidipijak di situ langitdijunjung*" (Wherever ground is stood on, the sky is hold high, meaning "respecting local culture and custom of where we are") is my priority and after arriving in Shanghai, my questions started to be answered one by one. It turned out that it was not as I worried.

The first day of my arrival at Shanghai Pudong International Airport, I was welcomed by a student taking me to SISU Foreign Expert Building where I stayed. Later, another student came and took me to open a bank account, to start using the local cell phone service, and to have lunch at a Moslem restaurant in a big mall. It was my first time that I had meal in Shanghai. The taste was very delicious and it was definitely halal.

The next day, I went to teach at Songjiang campus. I did not find any difficulty having halal food and practicing prayer. At the cafeteria, there was a room with halal food for Moslem. I could practice prayer as well in the room of the Indonesian Language Department because there was a sejadah (prayer rug) for praying. Students and lecturers extended me warm welcome and they helped me with everything so that I did not feel lonely.

The other day, I tried to look around near my neighborhood. Apparently, 20 meters from where I live, there is a Moslem restaurant offering complete and delicious Chinese food. There are not many Moslem restaurants in China, but there is usually one in every central avenue. A Chinese Moslem restaurant has some typical characteristics: there is a halal sign and the sellers usually wear white hat for men and black hijab for women. In addition, approximately 30 meters from my place, I also found an Arabian restaurant providing kebab, satay, and many more.

Near SISU Foreign Expert Building, there is a traditional market as well providing everything. I usually buy fruits there. Because I can not speak Chinese, when buying things, I only pay money in large notes and the seller would give me the change. They are nice and honest, always counting and selling based on the original prices. Supermarkets also sell imported products. I can find products of Thailand or Malaysia with halal label easily.

Because Moslems are a minority, it is quite difficult to find a mosque in the area where I live. I usually go to Huxi Mosque on Friday by taking Metro Line 3 from Chifeng Road Station to Zhenping Road Station and then walking for 15 minutes. Every Friday, the Huxi Mosque is crowded with Moslems practicing Friday prayer. At this mosque, I can easily buy various halal food and meat. Usually, I buy for one to two weeks supplies. At this very mosque I meet other Moslems from a lot of countries including China, Iran, Bangladesh, Malaysia, Pakistan, Turkey, and many more.

Today, it has been a month since I worked at SISU in Shanghai, China. I am very excited and have been truly enjoying living here. Up to this day, there is no significant problem that I have encountered as a Moslem living in China. One thing that I may suggest is that the university can provide special rooms for Moslems to practice prayer, for example, a musholla or surau (prayer house) at the university or faculty, because there are quite many Moslems studying and teaching at SISU.

Today, I am waiting for Ramadhan (fasting month) in China, because I will still be here when it comes. I am excited to experience fasting and doing Ramadhan prayer here.

About the author:

Nani Damayanti (Indonesian) graduated with a doctoral degree in linguistics from the University of Kebangsaan, Malaysia, lectures at Nipah University, and teaches Indonesian from February 2015 to July 2015 at the School of Asian and African Studies, SISU.

一位穆斯林教徒的中国行

Nani Darmayanti（印度尼西亚）

2015年3月至7月，我受工作单位帕查查兰大学（UNPAD）委派，至上海外国语大学东方语学院印尼语专业任教，教授印尼语。尽管此项目已开展十年，但我对此行还是充满担忧。此前，被委派过来任教的基本上都是男老师。而我是个戴穆斯林头巾的女性。来沪之前，很多问题萦绕在我的心头：我该如何用餐？如何做祷告？如何交流？如何与人交往？然而，作为一个印尼人，"*Di manabumidipijak di situ langitdijunjung*"[1]是我的第一信条。到上海后，我的问题一个接一个得以解决，原来事实并不像我担心的那样。

第一天抵达浦东国际机场后，一位上外学生迎接了我，并把我带到上外外国专家楼办理入住。之后，另一位学生带我去开通了银行账户和上海当地的手机号，还陪我去商场里的一家穆斯林餐馆用餐。那是我在上海的第一餐，十分美味并且绝对符合清真标准。

第二天，我去松江校区授课，在那儿吃到清真食品和做祷告没有一点困难。食堂有为穆斯林教徒专门准备的餐厅和清真食品。印尼语系的房间里也有穆斯林礼拜毯，我可以在那里做祷告。老师、学生们都热烈欢迎我，还事事帮助我，所以我一点也不感到孤独。

前几天，我试着到周边转转。距离我住处20米的地方，一个菜品美味丰富的穆斯林餐厅赫然在目。在中国，穆斯林餐厅并不多，通常每个中心街区都有一个，并有其典型特色：餐厅有清真标志，男店员通常戴白帽，女店员披黑头巾。此外，距离住所约30米处，我还发现一家供应土耳其烤肉、沙爹等美食的阿拉伯餐厅。

---

1 印尼谚语，直译："无论身处何地，天空仍旧高远"，引申义即"入乡随俗"。

我的住所附近还有一个传统菜市场，我常在那儿买水果。我不会说中文，买东西时我只能付大面额的纸币，再让商贩给我找零。他们人都很好而且诚实，算账都按原价。超市也供应进口商品，我可以轻易找到产自泰国或者马来西亚的清真食品。

　　因为穆斯林属于宗教少数群体，所以很难在我住的区域找到清真寺。通常每周五我会乘地铁3号线从赤峰路站上车，到镇坪路站下车出站再步行15分钟，就可以抵达沪西清真寺。每周五沪西清真寺里满是来做礼拜的穆斯林教徒。在那里，我很容易就能买到多种清真食品和清真肉品，一般买一到两个星期的用量。就在这座清真寺，我还能遇到来自中国、伊朗、孟加拉国、马来西亚、巴基斯坦、土耳其等国的穆斯林教徒。

　　现在，我来上外工作已经一个月了。我感到很欣慰，也很享受住在这里的时光。到今天为止，我这个在中国生活的穆斯林教徒还没遇到过什么大问题。不过我想提个建议：因为有众多穆斯林教徒在上外学习、授课，所以我希望学校专门为穆斯林教徒提供祷告的房间，比如在学校或者院系设立祷告室。

　　眼下我正在等待斋月的到来，因为届时我仍在中国。能在这里迎接斋月、做斋月祷告，是一件令人兴奋的事。

作者简介：

Nani Darmayanti（印度尼西亚籍）毕业于马来西亚国民大学语言学博士学位，是印尼巴查查兰大学教师，2015年2月至2015年7月期间被派往上海外国语大学东方语学院担任印尼语教师。

MY TRAVEL EXPERIENCE IN CHINA

Peter Andrew Christianson

Traveling is my passion, and I joke to my friends that traveling is to me what basketball is to Jeremy Lin. I've lived in Shanghai for over eight years, and people ask me why I have stayed here so long, and I tell them it's the abundance of travel opportunities in the area. Life in Shanghai has many stresses, but I feel refreshed after a trip out to one of the remote areas of China.

People ask me where I get the inspiration to travel to the obscure, remote places where I go, and I tell them there are many ways, often a combination of "red herring" and trial and error. I often go to places not too remote from Shanghai but that very few Shanghainese know about. And it goes without saying that almost every time the only foreigner I see on the trip is the one staring at me in the mirror of the hotel bathroom when I shave.

An example of this type of trip was a seeming misadventure in December. I had read on the Internet about Gezaoshan (阁皂山), a mountain in the city of Zhangshu (樟树) in Jiangxi province. I thought I absolutely had to see this place that was the mother mountain of an extinct sect of Buddhism, the Lingbao (灵宝) school that syncretized Buddhism, Daoism, and Confucianism.

I was extremely excited at the thought of the mysticism of a place that combine three major religions or philosophies. There was very little information online about the mountain, but I read there were many ancient buildings there.

So when I took an overnight train to Zhangshu I was horribly disappointed to discover that the mountain was barely a mole hill, and that the only buildings were less than thirty years old. There was nothing mystical about this place I'd traveled so far to see.

But that evening I saw an ad in my Jiangxi map for a mountain called Yuhuashan (玉华山) in a nearby town, and I got up at the crack of dawn the next day to travel to that mountain. It was an arduous trek to the top, but I was rewarded by a stark, almost lunar landscape, and a collection of old, atmospheric shrines that seemed like they were part of some forgotten Shangri-La.

This mysticism I had been vainly seeking at Gezaoshan I finally found at the second mountain. On the third day, I trekked to the neighboring city of Fengcheng (丰城), knowing nothing about the place in advance. Sometimes the places I visit are so obscure that there's very little about them online.

I bought a map at the local bookstore when I arrived, and I rented a car for the day, setting forth to the beautiful ancient village of Baimazhai (白马寨), a collection of beautifully and intricately carved stone row houses. My taxi driver then drove as fast as he could to Luoshan (罗山), a mountain in the south of the city.

I was nervous, because I had booked a ticket for the 7:30pm train from Zhangshu to Shanghai, and it was already afternoon. We snaked slowly up the gorgeous mountain, and at the top was one of the most beautiful villages I have seen in my life, a collection of historic orange adobe homes overlooking a valley from a fairy tale.

The village looked like a time warp from more than a hundred years ago. I ambled through the streets peering into the quaint houses, and then I ran as fast as I could up the hill above the village to visit the twin shrines of the mountain.

It's a sacred tradition for pilgrims and other visitors to that mountain to eat a vegetarian meal prepared by an old woman who runs a tiny restaurant next to the shrines. Not eating one of her meals is like visiting Paris, climbing the Eiffel Tower, but never sampling a croissant or a glass of Merlot.

Sadly, though, I had an evening train to catch, and time did not allow me to partake of that pleasurable tradition. Later, though, as we drove back to Zhangshu, I felt proud and content, happy that I had seen some of the loveliest places on the earth, places that few people have heard of and even fewer have been to.

Most of my trips are variations on this theme. In February I traveled to Heyuan (河源) in eastern Guangdong province, and I saw Hakka roundhouses that were as splendid as the loveliest medieval European castles. Some of the biggest and oldest roundhouses were not on the maps or online, and I only heard about them from visiting with the locals.

One morning I rose early and took a bus to Longchuan (龙川) County to climb Huoshan (霍山), a famous local mountain. But on the way back, I saw a sign advertising a village called Tuocheng (佗城), which proved to be an open-air museum of old Chinese architecture and buildings built by returned overseas Chinese in the 1920s that were a fusion of Western and Eastern styles. I spent almost five hours exploring the village and its environs, and I got back to my hotel late.

For trips like these examples I get peppered with questions: How did I decide to go there? How did I find out about a specific attraction? And I always have similar answers. The city was near another city I trekked to and enjoyed. I stumbled upon the city while trawling the Internet for travel destinations. Maybe there was one particular site to see in a city, but through word of mouth suggestion I ended up dashing from one historic site to another.

I take pride in comparing myself to the 1920s writer-explorers for the American magazine *National Geographic*. Like them, I venture out not knowing what I will find, just trusting that one site will somehow lead to another and that I will have a fascinating account of temples, villages, castles, and mountains. And with the weeks-long vacation coming up next month, I look forward to some more adventures in remote, obscure places.

About the author:

Peter Andrew Christianson (US) holds a double master's degree in History and Cultural Studies at University of London, and has been working in China since 1998.

我的中国之旅

Peter Andrew Christianson（美国）

旅行是我的激情所在。我曾跟朋友开玩笑说，旅行之于我，就好比篮球之于林书豪。现在，我已经在上海生活了八年之久。每当别人问起我为什么在这里待那么久，我会告诉他们是因为这里有太多旅行的机会。虽然在上海生活有着各种各样的压力，但是我总会在一次远足后神清气爽。

有人问我是如何找到那些遥远且毫不知名的地方去旅行的，我告诉他们有很多种方法，往往是"踏破铁鞋无觅处，得来全不费工夫"。我经常去的地方其实离上海并不远，但是连上海人都不大知道那些地方。不用说，几乎每次旅行中我所能看到的唯一的外国人就是在旅馆浴室里对着镜子刮胡子的自己。

12月，我经历了一次看似运气不佳的旅行。我事先在网上搜到江西省樟树市有一座阁皂山，据说它是灵宝派（佛教的一支失传宗派，融合了佛教、道教和儒教）的发源地。我觉得一定要去看看这个地方。

一想到这个地方融合了三种主要的宗教哲学体系，我就无比的兴奋。网上关于这座山的信息不多，但是我查到那里有很多古迹。

　　但是当我坐火车颠簸了整整一个晚上抵达目的地后，我极其失望地发现，那所谓的"山"仅仅是一个小土坡，而那些所谓的"古建筑"仅有不到30年的历史。我千里迢迢跋涉而来的这个地方没有任何神秘性可言。

　　当晚，我在江西地图上发现一则广告，宣传的是坐落在附近城镇的玉华山。第二天一大早，我就起床赶赴那个地方。登顶的过程异常艰辛，但我却看到了荒凉质朴、几乎和月球表面一样的苍茫景观，山中那些古老、神圣的宗教遗迹仿佛将我引入了被遗忘的香格里拉仙境。

　　在玉华山，我终于找到在阁皂山苦苦寻觅未果的神秘感。第三天，我在事先没有做任何准备功课的情况下来到邻近的丰城。有时，我探访的地方太过荒僻，乃至于很难在网上找到相关的信息。

　　到达丰城后，我在当地的书店买了一张地图，然后租了一辆车，向美丽的古镇白马寨驶去。一路上，我欣赏到许多雕筑精巧优美的连排石屋。之后，我的司机又以最快的速度开往位于城市南边的罗山。

　　我有点紧张，因为我已经订好了晚上7点半从樟树返沪的火车票，而现在已经是下午了。我们在壮丽的山上蜿蜒前行，抵达山顶后，我看到了这辈子所看到的最美丽的村庄景色之一：充满历史印记的黄色土坯居民村落俯瞰着整个山谷，宛如童话一般。

　　这个村子像是被历史尘封了一百多年。我漫步在街上，凝视着古色古香的房子，然后以最快的速度登山去看双神庙。

　　那里，香客和游客们会去庙宇旁边一个老妇人经营的素食餐厅吃饭，这是一个神圣的传统，不这样做的话就好比到巴黎看埃菲尔铁塔，却不去品尝羊角面包或红酒一样。

　　遗憾的是，由于急着赶晚上的火车，时间不允许我参加这个愉快的传统活动。尽管如此，在我们开车返回樟树的路上，我依然感到骄傲和满足，因为我欣赏到了一些世上最美丽的地方，一些鲜为人知、少有游客踏足的地方。

我的大多数旅行都是类似这样的探索。二月，我来到位于广东省东部的河源，看到了客家围屋，它们就如同欧洲中世纪最美的城堡一样壮观。一些最大、最古老的围屋只有在我探访当地人时才知晓，在地图或网络上压根就找不到相关信息。

一天，我起个大早乘车到龙川县游览霍山，这是当地的一座名山。在回来的路上，我看见广告牌宣传一个叫佗城的村子。这个地方就像是中国古建筑的露天博物馆，所有的建筑都是20世纪20年代的归国华侨修建的，它们融合了东西方不同的设计风格。我花了近五个小时探访这个村庄和它周边的地方，当我回到酒店时，天色已经很晚了。

对于这样的旅行，别人常问我各种问题：你为什么决定去那里？你是如何找到那些地方的？我的答案大同小异：那些地方要么是在某一个我长途跋涉去游览的城市附近，要么是我在上网时无意间发现的。也许最初我只想去看某个城市的某个景点，但是通过当地人的口口相传，我最终却接连去了好几个具有历史渊源的地方。

我很自豪地把自己跟20世纪20年代美国《国家地理》杂志的作家和探险家相比较。像他们一样，我对于旅行的终点一无所知，但我相信一个目的地将会把我引向另一个目的地，在众多神秘的寺庙、村庄、城池和山岭中领略精彩瞬间。下个月我即将迎来为期数周的假期，我期待着能够在某个遥远未知的地方展开更加奇妙的旅途。

作者简介：

Peter Andrew Christianson（美国籍）持有英国伦敦大学文化史和历史学双硕士学位，1998年来华工作至今。

A WEEKEND IN THE CLOUDS: HUANG SHAN

Raymond Kolter

During the past five years while teaching law in Shanghai, I have been fortunate enough to travel extensively throughout China, visiting many of the mainland provinces, even taking a boat to Hainan Island. I have climbed most of the holy mountains in China, from Mt. Changbai in the northeast to Mt. Wutai in the north, from Mt. Emei in the southwest to Mt. Tai in the east. It has been an incredible journey; riding camels across the Taklimakan and Gobi Deserts, herding sheep across the Tibetan Plateau, horseback riding on the steppes of Inner Mongolia and along the crystal blue shores of Qinghai Lake, even seeing a brilliant sunrise while cruising down the Yangtze River through the Three Gorges. Frequently I'm asked of all the many places in China I have visited, which I consider the most beautiful. It is indeed a difficult question to answer, but after much reflection, I feel Huang Shan (Yellow Mountain) was perhaps the most scenic and inspiring, truly a must-see in China.

Huang Shan is widely appreciated as the most beautiful mountain range in the country, with the cloud-covered peaks attracting scholars, poets, and artists over the centuries. It is situated in the southern portion of Anhui Province, bordering Jiangxi and Zhejiang Provinces. Its sharp, granite peaks form breathtaking vistas when seen jutting through the sea of clouds. The hiking trails can be either leisurely or strenuous, depending on your preference, and the cable car is available for those wishing to just sit back and view the rock formations and slopes covered with ancient, twisted pines. With names like Lion Peak, Celestial Capital Peak, and Begin-to-Believe Peak, the sights definitely live up to their titles. Once there, you will discover the inspiration for centuries of paintings found in Chinese museums. If you're lucky enough to see the sunrise over the clouds, you will undoubtedly find it one of the most memorable moments of your time spent in China.

About the author:

Raymond Kirk Kotler (US) graduated with a Doctoral degree from the School of Law, Pepperdine University and has been teaching at SISU since 2007.

云中的周末——黄山游记

Raymond Kolter （美国）

过去五年，我在上海担任法律教师，这期间，我很幸运能有机会在中国四处游览。我去过中国大陆很多省份，甚至坐船去过海南岛。我攀登过中国绝大多数的名山，从东北的长白山到华北的五台山，从西南的峨眉山到华东的泰山。我拥有很多神奇的经历，比如骑骆驼穿行于塔克拉玛干沙漠和戈壁滩，在青藏高原上放羊，骑在马背上徜徉在内蒙古草原和碧蓝的青海湖岸边，在三峡乘船而下时恰逢令人目眩的日出景象。经常有人问我，在这么多我去过的地方中，哪里最美？这的确很难回答，但是仔细回想后，我觉得黄山也许是我去过的风景最壮美的地方了，这里也是来中国的必去景点。

黄山被誉为中国最美的山。它云雾缭绕的山峰吸引了历代文人墨客和艺术家。它坐落在安徽省的南部，邻近江苏省和浙江省。茫茫云海中，那陡峭嶙峋的山峰散发出摄人心魄的美。登山的过程可以很轻松，也可以很艰苦，这取决于你的选择。山上配有缆车，是专为那些想惬意享受奇石美景以及古老奇松的游客们准备的。大名鼎鼎的狮子峰、天都峰、始信峰，都是实至名归。在黄山，你会找到博物馆中陈列的古老山水画的灵感源泉。如果你足够幸运，有机会看到云海日出，那这无疑将成为你在中国最值得纪念的时刻。

作者简介：

Raymond Kirk Kolter（美国籍）毕业于美国佩珀代因大学法学博士学位，2007年来华工作至今，现为上海外国语大学法学院教师。

CHINA AS I SEE IT

Tanomwong Lamyodmakpol

Thammasat University and SISU have had an exchange program in place since 2002. In 2005, I began teaching at the School of Asian and African Studies as a foreign expert specializing in Thai language and literature. It's been a decade now. Although I wasn't the first international member of staff, I was the first to apply to teach at SISU. Ever since I arrived at SISU, although I didn't come every term, I did go to SISU more often than other teachers from the liberal arts department at Thammasat.

SISU is laid out in a similar way to Thammasat: a smaller campus over 80km^2 in the city's older district, and a larger one over 100km^2 in the suburbs. The Hongkou campus is comparable therefore to Thammasat's Tha Pra Chan campus, and Songjiang is like Rangsit. The international faculty at SISU live in Hongkou. On days when I had class, I would walk about 600 metres to take the coach to the other campus, where I taught.

The journey took about an hour each way. No matter whether it was in the morning or evening, everyone fell asleep almost as soon as they got on — the journey was more strenuous than teaching, and took more time too.

My parents have many Chinese friends, a fact which has attracted me to China since I was a child. My family and I ate at Chinese restaurants, and ate snacks and fruits imported from China, such as salted plums, water chestnuts and Chinese chestnuts. I was a real foodie back then, although I didn't eat very much. I think that no matter which era it is, Chinese food always goes down well with the Thais. This is because even if food is cooked in traditional Chinese ways, the sauces used are appreciated in Thailand, such as Teo Cheow noodles which come in dozens of flavours.

I'm a person of simple habits when it comes to food, but sometimes I'm not so simple. I prefer fruit and vegetables to meat. I don't eat beef, because cows help us till the land; and I don't eat lamb. I eat pork and a bit of chicken. I often eat fish. So on the whole, I eat mostly fruit and vegetables. China is heaven for vegetable lovers. Personally I like peaches, plums, cherries, strawberries, blackcurrants, mulberries, pears, pomegranates, loquats and lychees. These are all seasonal; I'm not a great fan of the sort that last and that you can put in the fridge all year round. I like rice, whether it's Chinese or Thai; I like the sort that looks a bit darker than the ordinary type when it's cooked. I also like sweet corn, despite the fact it sells for 3 to 5 yuan per cob. Chinese spicy sauce is good too; the mother-in-law of one of my former students makes her own, and it tastes wonderful. You can't go without raw ginger either, because it's good for the circulation and makes you feel warmer in the depth of winter. The pickled ginger sold at E-mart is great; a Chinese teacher colleague gave me some ginger pickled in vinegar that her mother made and it was delicious. It went really well with a bit of porridge.

As for accommodation, the two important factors are the climate, and gardens. There are four seasons in China — spring, summer, autumn (the windy season) and winter, all of which are very different. I like spring most of all, because at the beginning you still have the coolness of winter and the long-awaited flower buds are just waiting to burst forth with life.

The flowers in the flowerbeds in Beijing and Shanghai blossom with equal beauty. Unfortunately there were always a lot of people who went to admire the flowers. The whole family — parents and grandparents on both sides — took their children or grandchildren, sometimes in strollers. In this way, my attempt to admire the flowers turned into admiring the children, who were cuter than the flowers. They will grow up one day, and then grow old much later on. The flowers however wither very quickly. Sometimes you can miss the moment when the flowers are in bloom, and there are only a few flowers left in the flowerbeds that haven't withered completely. Some trees specially planted as decoration become props in people's photographs.

On holidays, the parks were all full of visitors, so if I wanted to admire the flowers instead of the people, I had to go on an ordinary work day. For instance, Luxun Park, which is opposite SISU, was full of life: every month I used to visit the museum of the great writer Lu Xun — about six times in total. Almost every time, I would buy some postcards and leaflets or cheap art, as well as small notebooks at 40 yuan for a pack of five and with a cartoon by Feng Zikai on every page. In these I would write down my experiences, or things I'd seen on television and was worried I'd forget.

From August 2013 to the following year, Luxun Park was closed for renovation. I was then forced to go to Quyang Park, which is smaller but still nicely laid out. The first time I walked there and back; later I would go one stop on the bus and then walk back. The other parks I visited were all further away and I needed my Chinese students to take me, so I only went once. Both SISU campuses have areas that are similar to parks, but aren't proper parks. I don't think SISU had any plans to build such a park. I was a student from 2010 to 2011 at Peking University. I lived on the campus, which used to be part of the imperial gardens. Next to the hotel where I lived was a pond full of lilies, a disused garden and pavilion, and a twenty-metre-long path that allowed visitors to look at the old pavilion, which had perhaps not been repaired or done up. The advantage of the place was that there were trees and birds of all colours: black and grey, and with nests up in the trees. Almost every day I would buy food to feed the birds. Sometimes I would feed horses or dogs.

People who have visited Peking University may know how the groundsmen make full use of the surrounding environment to make things stand out and look better. There are two flowerbeds I liked the most: one is opposite the Shaoyuan building, inside the entrance that is open to vehicles only. The area has peonies which in winter have only faded stems, but which in spring bring forth brightly coloured, beautiful flowers. The other is in front of the dean's building, with the foreign faculty building on the right. There was a sort of flower there; I don't know the name, with a single layer of petals and many different colours. It reminded me of the silk robes worn by a princess or the kind of fairy who comes to this world in order to encourage the poor student studying hard for the civil service exams. I had never seen these two sorts of flowers at either the Hongkou or Songjiang campuses until one day in the spring of 2013 when I went to the greenhouse behind Teaching Building No.1 and saw a clump of huge peonies. They were in bloom, in purple. I really liked them so I took a photo on the spot and told other people about the flowers so they could come and admire them too. Most of the people at SISU walk or ride their bicycles on the main path, so many of them missed this bunch of flowers hidden away behind the building.

Although there aren't the perfect sort of flowers that I had hoped for at SISU, I liked the trees there very much. I also think that I might actually know more about these trees than the Chinese do. On my days off, I sometimes went to Songjiang in order to walk and enjoy the sunshine (there aren't many trees there) and keep fit, and to train my long-distance vision. I went there because there was more green to see than in the city, and in order to feed the birds (in winter, most of the birds migrate south — some to Thailand). Spring was the best time to get back in touch in nature; sometimes one of the teachers, who is Chinese and who teaches Farsi, would come up to and say hello. One day he took me to see the pomelo trees in front of the Japanese department. I just tasted pomelo for the first time this year and came to the conclusion that it's not really suitable for eating. Another time, he took me to see a plum tree. The leaves were purple. Because the leaves and fruit were a similar colour, I never realized a plum bore fruit. I tried one; it was sour and very tasty. Behind the Department of Asian and African Studies building there were many orange trees. I liked them best when they were in bloom and gave off their faint scent, so I often went to smell them. Last year however I picked some and they were really sour. The Chinese don't eat them like that but in Thailand people like that sour taste. So I plucked some and squeezed them for the juice, then mixed the juice with honey. It wasn't only tasty — it was rich in Vitamin C. I like the orange trees here because I can be certain they haven't been exposed to pesticide or fertilizer. At the time there were many oranges on the tree, but one day they all disappeared. Perhaps the groundsmen took them all. They probably wouldn't eat them so it's a real pity.

Looking around the surroundings of the teaching building, there were many plants particularly romantic because of their little yellow flowers (yellow is my personal colour). When the petals have all withered, a round seed is exposed. If there is a strong wind, the little seeds at the tip are carried into the air where they float about. I liked to ruffle the flowers and watch the seeds disperse in the wind. In 2013, I found out from a Japanese TV program that dandelion petals can relieve inflammation and treat stomach ailments. Dandelion works with salad or as a tea; so on mornings when the weather was good, I would pick some dandelions (what I call "liontooth grass") and eat them. However, sometimes the groundsmen ignored the fact that these plants can be eaten or used as medicine, and that they are beautiful things that should be used to decorate the school, and just got rid of them. There is another plant I absolutely have to mention: because even if you've never seen it, you will definitely have smelled it — cassia. These were well taken care of by the groundsmen and their scent was everywhere on both campuses. The fragrance of these little yellow flowers enveloped the whole city. Behind the Lu Xun memorial museum, there are two or three orange coloured cassias that I suspect few apart from the gardeners have ever seen. Another flower I had to admire every time was the magnolia. There is a pair of these at the Lu Xun mausoleum, and even more at SISU. Behind the SISU Press and by the Hongkou campus canteen there are many pink and purple little flowers in bloom, while the larger trees only blossom in June.

The SISU Hotel, where I lived, is owned by the university but is situated about 600 metres away. Therefore, I had to walk to the fountain on campus and take the coach to Songjiang. No matter how cold the weather was, or how dark and deserted it was, I would shoulder my bag packed with books, homework and my lunch and walk over. I had to take the coach at that time because there was no later service, perhaps due to a desire on the part of the government to cut expenses or reduce pollution. Each stop on a bus route in China is far away from the others. Although there is a bus stop near to the SISU Hotel, the terminus is about 800 metres away from the university. During my first year in Shanghai, the SISU Hotel had just been renovated. I was the first guest to stay in my room there so I had to give it a thorough clean. I have an allergy, so in order to breathe better I had to wipe away the shavings and sawdust left by the decorators. During my first month there, the weather was still pretty hot. It was only when autumn arrived that I realized there was no indoor heating and that there would probably be none for the next ten years. During the winter therefore, when the temperature was minus seven degrees Celsius or even lower, I had to wear three layers of clothing, a hat, and very thick shoes. I would sleep clutching a hot-water bottle or under an electric blanket. If it was even colder I would sleep on the sofa in the lobby, because it was warmer than in the bedrooms. There was only one channel with clear reception and good sound — NHK. That's what I remember of my accommodation — I was proud of my ability to adapt.

SISU calls its foreign faculty "Foreign Language Experts", which sounds pretty cool. I was confident about my job. It was important to make a good impression on your colleagues and the students here, because you often saw them around. There were two absolutely lovely female teachers who helped me out a lot. They would take me shopping, or out to eat delicious food, or on trips everywhere. They gave me cakes and traditional holiday food. When I was down they would give me support and encouragement. Those days were the exception; I was good at getting back to normal so I won't go into the details. There was one thing that made me want to return home however: some of the students didn't apply themselves; they wouldn't bother handing in homework or would skip class. These things might appear like a good thing because they reduced my workload, but as a teacher I had no right to feel that way about it. It was at least a comfort to think that the majority of my students were very diligent, did most of their homework, and turned up. For me, to be able to travel three thousand miles from my home all alone to Shanghai, and gain a wealth of experience — not just in teaching Thai — this was enough.

I have not kept in touch with many of my students from the first four years, but there are still several who have never forgotten me — and I will never forget them. These continuing relationships are both cause and product of my many visits to China. Because of the efforts of our Princesses Maha Chakri Sirindhorn and Chulabhorn Walailak, the friendship between our nations is greater. Teaching Thai language, literature and culture, as well as holding a diverse range of different events, will all help us Thais create a good impression of Thailand in the eyes of the Chinese. It's just like the way my Chinese friends and students have given me a wonderful impression of China — an impression that has drawn me time and again to China.

I can't hope to see the whole country for myself, so I can't talk about everything to do with this country. Over the coming months, I will "visit" China in my thoughts. I may no longer be in China but every wonderful memory will remain with me — and those unhappy parts will remain as a character-building part of my experience.

About the author:

Tanomwong Lamyodmakpol (Thai) graduated with a doctorate in literature and art from Florida State University. She is currently a professor at the Faculty of Liberal Arts at Thammasat University. From

2012 to 2014, Lamyodmakpol taught Thai at the School of Asian and African Studies, SISU.

我眼中的中国

Tanomwong Lamyodmakpol（泰国）

　　法政大学从2002年就与上外有合作交流项目，我自2005年开始以泰国语言文学专家的身份来到上外东方语学院泰语系，算到今年也有10年了。尽管我不是第一个外教，我也算是第一个提出申请来上外担任外教的人（但没能第一个来）。自从我来上外任教以来，虽然并不是每个学期都来，但也是比法政大学文学院的其他外教来得要频繁些。

　　上外校园和法政大学有着相似之处：上外包括占地八万余平方米的规模较小的老校区和在市郊十余万平方米的规模较大的新校区，于是就可以将虹口校区与法政的Tha Pra Chan校区作比，将松江校区与Rangsit校区作比。上外外教的住宿区位于虹口。在有课的日子，我就走六百米左右去搭乘市区校区的班车，为的就是到市郊的校区教课。每次大约都要花一个小时左右，不论是早上或是傍晚，大家一上车几乎都昏昏沉沉地睡着了，因为旅途的疲惫要胜过教书的辛劳，所花费的时间也要比教书的时间要多。

　　因为我的父母有很多中国亲友，所以中国是一个我从孩提时代就想去的国家。我们在中国餐厅吃饭，吃从中国运来的点心和水果，比如咸话梅、荸荠和栗子。当年的我是个吃客，虽然吃得不多。我觉得中国人不管在什么时代做的食物都很符合泰国人的口味。因为他们即便用的是中国传统的烹饪方式，也用上了泰国人喜欢的调料，比如潮州粉条就有几十种口味。

我是个饮食简单的人，但有时也吃得复杂。喜食蔬果胜过食肉。不吃牛肉，因为牛助人们耕田；不吃羊肉；吃猪肉和一点鸡肉，通常吃鱼肉；大多还吃些蔬果。中国是喜爱各种蔬菜的人的天堂。至于我喜欢的水果，有桃子、李子、樱桃、草莓、黑加仑、桑葚、香梨、石榴、枇杷和荔枝，这些都是时令水果。至于一年四季都有的水果，那些放在冰箱里整年都可以吃到的水果，我就不太喜欢。我喜欢吃米饭，不论是中国的还是泰国的大米都喜欢，喜欢煮出来后颜色比普通大米要深的米饭；也喜欢玉米，尽管每根玉米要三到五元钱。中国的辣椒酱也很好吃，我一个学生的丈母娘自家制作的更是美味。生姜更是不可缺少的蔬菜，因为它能促进血液循环，也会让人在寒冷的季节里感觉到温暖；在易买得买到的腌生姜是称心的美味，中国教师给我带来的自家母亲亲自腌制的老醋姜也很好吃，佐稀饭共食，让人感觉愉悦。

关于住的方面，首先就要讲到气候和花园。中国有四个季节，分别是春、夏、秋（即风季）和冬，每个季节有各自鲜明的天气特点。我最喜欢春季，因为开始时还伴着未退的凉意，而等候已久的花骨朵也蓄势待发，绽放得热烈起来。北京和上海的花圃里花绽放得一样漂亮，但去赏花的时候，总是会有很多人。爸爸妈妈爷爷奶奶外公外婆抱着儿女牵着孙子或是推着儿童车来赏花，于是我去赏花就变成是去观赏那些比花还要美的孩子们。孩子们会长大成人，过很久以后老去，而花开不久就会凋零。有时候去赏花没能赶上花朵盛开，那花圃里只剩下几株还没落尽的花，而也有几处花圃里有为了装饰用而特别种下的树，专供人们拍照。

在休息日，每处公园里都有很多前来观光游览的人，因此，如果是要去看花而不是去看人，就得在平时的工作日去。就比如位于上外对面的鲁迅公园，这个公园很有生机，我每月都会去鲁迅纪念馆拜祭伟大的中国作家——鲁迅，至今已去过大约六次，几乎每次去都会买一些明信片、书目介绍或是廉价艺术品，也会买小的笔记本，每套五本，40元，每一页上都印有丰子恺画的漫画，我买来记录我亲身经历的事情，或是那些我从电视上看到的怕会遗忘的见闻。

2013年的8月到2014年的8月，鲁迅公园关闭进行整修，我就必须去比鲁迅公园小但是也布置得很好的曲阳公园，第一次去是步行往返，后来我就坐车乘一站路去然后走回来。至于我去过的一些其他的公园距离都很远，必须得有中国学生陪同，所以我都只去过一次。在上外的两个校区都有类似公园但其实并非公园的区域，我觉得上外并没有建造我印象里所谓公园的计划。2010到2011年间，我在北京大学求学，我的住处就在这个曾是皇家园林的校园里，在所住的宾馆旁边有荷花池、废弃的园子和亭子，从一条20米长的小道上就可以望见那座年久失修的亭子。在这样的小园子里，好的地方就在于有树和各种颜色的鸟，有黑色的、灰色的，在树梢筑有鸟巢。我几乎天天都会买食物来喂鸟，有时候也会喂马、喂狗。

曾去过北京大学的人可能曾感受过园丁充分利用周围环境来衬托和美化景物的园林技巧。那里的中式花圃中我最喜欢的有两处：一处位于勺园的对面，在那个机动车专用门的内侧，那里有牡丹，在冬天只能看见褐色的根，而在春天就会长出斑斓而美丽的花朵；另一处位于校长楼的前面，右边是外教们的办公楼——外文楼，在那里有一种不知名的花，有单层的花瓣，花有好几种颜色，让人想起公主或者传说中下凡鼓励为了考取状元而勤奋读书的农村穷书生的仙女穿的丝绸霓裳。这两种花我在虹口或是松江都不曾见，直到2013年春天的一天，我走到虹口一号教学楼后面的育苗室，看见了一簇很大的牡丹，开出的花是紫色的，我很欣喜，立刻拍下了照片，并告诉别人这个消息让他们也来赏花。上外人步行或是驾车大多都是在更宽阔的大马路上，而这花隐蔽地掩藏在楼背后，所以很多人不曾见过。

　　虽然上外没有我理想中的花圃，但我很喜欢上外的树，也觉得相比起中国人来，我可能更了解中国的树。在没有课的日子里，有时候我也会去松江，为的是去散步和享受阳光（那儿较少树木遮蔽）以保持健康，也为的是纵目远眺（那儿能比在城市里看到更多的绿色）；另一方面也是为了喂鸟（冬季，鸟大多向南迁移，有一些会飞去泰国）。春季是最适合亲近大自然的时节，有几天也会有教波斯语的中国老师走来，边走边向我打招呼。有一天他带我去日语学院楼前面看柚子树，我今年刚尝过那柚子，得出的结论是不太适合拿来吃。还有一天他带我去看李子树，叶子是紫色的，因为叶子的紫色和果子的紫色相像，我一直不知道它还会结果子，我尝了一个，酸酸的很可口。在东方语学院教学楼的后面有好几株橙子树，我最喜欢橙子树开花的清香，于是经常去闻，但去年我去摘了些来尝，却是特别的酸。中国人对这不感兴趣，但泰国人喜欢酸的口味，于是我就去采了来榨汁，和蜂蜜调在一起食用，不仅好吃，还补充了维C。我喜欢这里的橙子，因为肯定没有农药，也没有施化肥。那时树上还结了很多的橙子，但有一天就全部不见了，可能是被园丁全摘下来了，他们或许也不会拿去食用，真是可惜了。

　　当我望向教学楼周围的大地，就能看见好些特别浪漫的植物，因为开出的是小小的黄色小花（黄色是我的生辰色），当花瓣落尽，就能看到球形的种子，若是大风吹来，位于末端的细小种子就会被风带着旋转着飘散。我喜欢将那些种子，好让它们随风飘散。2013年的时候，我从日本电视台得知这蒲公英的叶子可以去内热，还可以治胃疾，用来拌色拉或是冲茶都行，于是在天气好的早晨，我就去采摘蒲公英（我把它们叫做"狮牙草"）来吃。但有时园丁尽管知道它们是可用于药食的植株，也是美丽的花朵，可以拿来装饰校园，他们也会把蒲公英清除掉。除此之外，还有一种植物必须提一下，因为即便你不曾看到它，你也一定会闻到它的香，那就是桂花。因为园丁的悉心照料，桂花得以香遍两个校区。整个上海都会被这种好心肠的黄色小花的香气笼罩。在鲁迅博物馆的后面，有两三株橙色的桂花，除了园丁之外大概也没几个人见过。还有一种我每次看见都要欣赏一番的花是玉兰花，在鲁迅墓有两株成对的大玉兰树，而在上外就更多了，在出版社的后面和虹口的食堂边有早早绽放的粉色、紫色的小花，至于那些大树，要到6月方会开花。

上外宾馆是隶属于上外的宾馆，但位于校区之外约600米的地方，而我每次都要走到喷泉处搭乘班车，无论天气再怎么冷，路再怎么黑怎么冷清，我都要背起装着书本、作业和午餐的包走过去，因为晚些时间就没有班车了，这可能是政府为了节省开支、减少污染的缘故。中国的公交车站相隔都很远。尽管在所住的上外宾馆附近就有公交站，但终点站距离学校大约就有800米的距离。我第一年来的时候，上外宾馆刚刚改建装修，我是我所住的那间房间的第一个旅客，因而必须仔细地打扫。因为我过敏的缘故，为了顺畅呼吸，就要擦除锯木头留下的碎屑和施工带来的粉尘。来到这里的第一个月天还挺热的，等到了秋天才知道这里没有暖气供应，在接下来的十年里或许也不会有，因此在冬天，室温将近零下7度甚至更低，必须穿三件衣服，戴帽子，穿很厚的鞋。睡觉的时候要抱着热水袋或是用电热毯来驱寒。若是更冷，就要睡在客厅的沙发上，因为会比睡在小房间里暖些。我所能听懂的声音清晰、画质清楚的电视频道只有一个——日本的NHK频道。这些是我印象里关于居住的事，我对自己适应环境的能力感到骄傲。

上外把外教们称作外国语专家，听上去很酷。工作上我很自信。在这里工作也须得给共事的老师们和所教的学生们留下好的印象，因为会经常碰到他们。有两个女教师非常可爱，帮了我很多忙，比如带我去买东西，带我去吃美味佳肴，带我到处游览，还给我带点心和节日食物，在我苦闷的日子里给了我很大的鼓舞和力量。苦闷的日子不常有，我也能很快地调整心情，在此也就不一一详述。只一件事让我有想回家的冲动，就是有些学生不认真学习，不交作业、翘课。这些事情看起来好像是好事，因为好像能让我减少些工作量，但作为一名教师，是不能够因为这样的事而感到开心满意的。能让我舒缓郁结的，就是想到大多数的学生学习都很刻苦，常做作业，也不缺课。对于一个孤身一人离家三千多英里来此生活，还得到许多教授泰语以外的经历的人来说，这些就够了。

前四届的学生大多已不再和我有联系了，但也有些不曾忘记我，我也永远不会忘记他们，因为这种牵挂和联系是我数次造访中国的原因与成果。中泰两国之间因为诗灵通公主和朱拉蓬公主的努力而发展了深厚的友谊。教授泰语技能、泰国文学、泰国文化并开展多种多样的活动，都是为了让泰国人和泰国在中国人的眼中留下美好的印象，正如同我的中国朋友和学生们代表中国给我留下了美好的印象一样，这种美好让我一次又一次地造访中国。

我的双眼无法看遍整个中国，也就使得我无法尽述所有的事。在接下来的日子里，我会用"心"去看。当我不在中国的时候，中国的那些美好的点点滴滴也将永远留在我的心里，而那些曾让我不开心的事情，我也会当作是我在中国的有益的经历。

作者简介：

Tanomwong Lamyodmakpol（泰国籍）毕业于美国佛罗里达州立大学阅读与文学艺术博士学位，现为泰国国立法政大学文学院教授，于2012-2014年期间担任上海外国语大学东方语学院泰语系教师。

三、学习篇

RINGTONE SERVICE

Elizabeth H. Geiger

A confession. When I arrived to teach in Fuzhou, China in 2013, I was still not a smartphone person. I liked my stupid phone, a little mobile that had traveled through many countries with me without complaint.

But for only 200 RMB, I took the plunge — a Lenovo. Four days later, it was stolen. My solace? I was one of very few Westerners in Fuzhou, and I just kept imagining the look on the thief's face when he turned the phone over and, instead of the expected Apple, discovered he had stolen a bottom-of-the-heap Lenovo. Back to my stupid phone I went.

When I arrived to teach in Shanghai in 2014, I was told that my life here would be an utter disaster without WeChat. So with my new phone plan, I got a brand-spanking-new Lenovo. Problem was, over the next day or two, I discovered that several people had called or texted me, but the phone never rang. I showed it to a particularly geeky guy, and he confirmed what I had sort of discovered: there were no ringtones on it.

I took the phone back to China Mobile, but this time the lovely guy who had sold it to me, and spoke English, wasn't there. They put me on the line with an English-speaking customer service rep. I explained my problem, and she said, "Oh, you want our ringtone service."

"No," I said, "I just want a phone that rings."

"So, you want our ringtone service."

"No, just a phone that..."

And back and forth we went. Finally, I said, "Look, I'm old. Work with me here. I remember when phones didn't do a lot of things, but they rang. Please, just make this one ring." She had me put the guy in the store back on the line. He gave me a choice of three little tunes. I picked the least offensive. He downloaded it, and off I went.

Or so I thought. Later that day I discovered that the phone rang when people called me, but was silent when they texted me. I looked, and sure enough, no messaging ringtones. Back to China Mobile. This time they put me on the line with a different English-speaking service rep. I told her my sad story, and she said, "Oh, you want our messaging ringtone service."

"No, I just want it to make some kind of noise when somebody texts me."

"So, you want our messaging ringtone service."

"No, I just..."

Back and forth. Back and forth. And then, "Look, I'm old. Work with me here. I remember when phones..." At long last, she had me put the guy in the store back on the line. He downloaded. And, finally, I had a phone that made all the appropriate noises.

It has become a frequent refrain with my colleagues:

"Oh, you want the cross-on-green service."

"Oh, you want the registering-your-apartment-with-only-one-trip-to-the-police-station service."

"Oh, you want the key with the unlocking-door service."

"Oh, you want the passengers-off-before-passengers-on subway service."

"Oh, you want the pencil sharpener with the pencil-sharpening service."

And on it goes. Could anyone tell me when this will ever end?

About the author:

Elizabeth Helen Geiger (US) graduated with a Master's Degree on Drama History / Theory and Criticism from the College of Hunte, NYU and is teaching at the Overseas Training Centre, SISU.

手机铃声服务

Elizabeth H. Geiger （美国）

我承认，当我2013年刚到福州教书的时候，我还不太会用智能手机。我喜欢我笨笨的旧手机，尽管它很小，但是它跟着我旅行过很多国家，从未出现过任何问题。

但是，当我看到售价仅200元的联想手机时，我心动了。短短4天后，这个手机就被偷了。我只有苦中作乐：作为福州极少数西方人中的一个，我时不时地幻想着那个小偷把我的手机翻过来时发现自己仅偷到一个非常陈旧的联想手机（而非他所期待的苹果手机）时脸上的囧样。没办法，我又开始用起了以前的旧手机。

2014年，我来到上海任教。人们告诉我，如果不用微信，我的生活将会一团糟。这次，通过新办的手机套餐，我得到了一部崭新的联想手机。问题是，在接下来的一两天里，尽管有很多人给我打过电话或者发过短信，但是我的手机却从来不响。我把手机给一个技术男看，他验证了我之前无意中的发现：这个手机没有铃声。

我把手机带到了中国移动的营业厅。上次将手机卖给我的那个会讲英语的可爱小伙子刚好不在，于是他们让我给提供英语服务的热线打电话。我跟工作人员解释了手机的问题，她说："哦，那么你需要订购我们的来电铃声服务。"

"不，"我说，"我只要我的手机能响。"

"那么你还是需要订购我们的来电铃声服务。"

"不，我只想要一个手机能……"

我们就这样争论了好几个来回。最后我说："你看，我上了岁数。你就通融一下吧。我年轻的时候，手机可能没有其他功能，但是它肯定会响铃。你就让我的手机能响吧！"于是，她让我去找另外一个小伙子，他给了我三种不同的铃声选择，我选了一个听上去最柔和的，他帮我下载好，然后我就离开了。

我以为这样就万事大吉了。之后我发现，当有人打我电话的时候，手机确实响了，但是当有人给我发短信时，手机仍然不响。我看了一下，果然，我的手机没有短信铃声。于是我又回到中国移动的营业厅。这一次，他们让我去给另一个提供英语服务的热线打电话。我将我的悲惨遭遇又讲述了一遍，她说："哦，那么你需要订购我们的短信铃声服务。"

"不，"我说，"我只想要我的手机在收到短信时能响。"

"那么你还是需要订购我们的短信铃声服务。"

"不，我只是……"

就这样，我们又争论了好几个来回，然后我说："你看，我上了岁数。你就通融一下吧。我年轻的时候……"最后，她让我去找另外一个小伙子，他帮我下载了铃声。终于，我有了一个能适时发出各种声音的手机。

类似移动客服回答的各种"新奇"评论现在已经成为了我和同事之间的"口头禅"：

"哦，那你需要订购'行人过马路绿灯行'服务。"

"哦，那你需要订购派出所《外国人临时住宿登记单》[1]一站式服务。"

"哦，那你需要订购能提供开门服务的钥匙。"

"哦，那你需要订购'地铁乘客先下后上'服务。"

"哦，那你需要订购能提供削铅笔服务的铅笔刀。"

我不禁问道：这样的无休无止何时才是个头呢？

作者简介：

Elizabeth Helen Geiger（美国籍）毕业于纽约市立大学亨特学院戏剧史/理论与批评硕士学位，现为上海外国语大学出国培训部教师。

1　译者注：我国《外国人入境出境管理条例》规定，境外人员在城镇住宿，须于抵达后24小时内，由留宿人或本人持住宿人的证件和留宿人的户口簿到当地公安机关申报，开具临时住宿登记表。

CHINESE WEIRDO

George Fleming

The first time I gave some serious thought to studying Chinese was when I was 17. It was my secondary school French teacher who got me thinking about the idea. One day, when we had finished our class work, he began chatting to us and the topic turned to China. That day my teacher talked about China's economic rise, but what got me interested was the language, culture and history. From that moment on I decided to devote some serious time to following events in China. The first book about the country that I read was Jung Chang's *Wild Swans: Three Daughters of China*, which had a really big effect on me. I decided to study Chinese. There were about 150 students in my year at school. When it came to university applications, most people chose "normal" subjects — I don't remember that many applications for modern languages, and of the few students who did apply, they would apply for German and French, or French and Italian. At the time, when my classmates found out I was going to study Chinese at university, they had the same expression of disbelief or confusion: "Why would you want to study *that?*" Other than myself, there was one other guy who opted for something rather out of the ordinary (Arabic). I suspect we were held to be the official weirdoes of our school year. When I told my family I wanted to study Chinese, they were initially very surprised, but when they saw how resolute I was quickly gave me a lot of support. I remember my mother saying how when she was at school, China seemed as far away as the moon to most people.

People often talk about the richness of Chinese culture, and this is absolutely true. The first place I stayed in China was Qingdao, where I taught at a bilingual kindergarten in 2006. Later on I studied at Ocean University of China (also in Qingdao) on my half-year abroad. Even now when I hear the local accent, it takes me back to that time. After my undergraduate I came to SISU to study interpretation and translation. Learning is an infinite process — the more you learn, the more aware of the limits of your knowledge you become.

China is a huge country with huge differences between regions in language, diet and customs. For me this is both challenging and fascinating. In this one country, you can learn lots of different languages and meet all kinds of people and make friends. The karaoke clubs have songs in Mandarin, English, Hokkien and Cantonese. I'm interested in a wide spectrum of different music — everything from staunchly Beijing-proud underground rap groups like IN3 to the classic pop kings and queens like Jacky Cheung or Fish Leong, to Taiwanese rocker Wu Bai. For cuisine here in Shanghai, you can nip out in the middle of the night for lamb kebabs and a beer; or you can try Shaanxi's wide, flat *biangbiang* noodles, local Shanghainese, Cantonese *dim sum*, or for Sichuanese, hot pot or marinated chicken.

If I had to describe one thing the Chinese have in common... their hospitality. No matter whether I am in Harbin, Beijing, Shanghai or Changsha, I am warmly received. People are very outgoing here and ready to make friends. It's great. If I have to mention something that's not so good, it's the regional divisions here. People from different places around China, to the smallest place, are very proud of their hometown. This pride has its downside: it leads to an us-and-them attitude to outsiders. I hope that in the future more Chinese can live and work around China, and experience life in, and get to know more people, from other places.

The past few years in Shanghai have been good. Shanghai is both a modern international city and a place with a lot of history. I like going for a jog in the mornings and often run to the Bund. Along the way, I pass many old buildings. There are a lot of things in Shanghai that we don't really have back home — for instance, Puzzle Rooms. These code-cracking games range from the very basic to sophisticated, grand places. I find them fascinating. There are few puzzle rooms in London but this form of entertainment is nowhere near as well-established as in Shanghai. I like tackling the codes and puzzles at these places with friends, although I must admit I'm not the strongest mathematician compared to my Chinese friends, so I'm not sure how much of a contribution I actually make! These rooms remind me a bit of a TV series that was on when I was little, *The Crystal Maze*.

Chinese literature is another immensely rich facet of its culture. There are simply too many books I want to read — from ancient Tang fantasy stories, to the great novels like *Dream of the Red Chamber*, to modern romance and kungfu novels. Ever since I became a translator I have wanted to introduce these amazing aspects of Chinese culture to the people back home. I hope that in the future I can contribute to this in some small way. I also hope my students can learn more about British culture.

About the author:

George Fleming (British) studied Chinese language and history at Cambridge University for his undergraduate degree before moving to Shanghai to pursue a postgraduate in interpretation and translation at SISU. He then became a full-time translator for three years, before (re)joining the translation department at the Graduate Institute of Interpretation and Translation, SISU, to teach Chinese-English translation.

学习中文的怪咖

费祖志（英国）

我第一次认真考虑学习中文是在我17岁的时候，当时的高中法语老师让我产生了这一想法。那天的课堂练习做完了，他跟我们聊天时讲起中国来。他讲的是中国的经济崛起，而对我而言，中国的语言、文化与历史更有意思。我从那一刻开始决定花点工夫关注中国的发展。我看的第一本关于中国的书是张戎的《鸿：三代中国女人的故事》，对我影响很大。我就下定决心学中文。当时高中那一届有大概150个学生，考的大学专业都比较主流，我印象中考外语的不多，就算考，那也是考个德—法语、法—意语专业吧。当时，很多同学听到我要上大学学习中文的时候，都会用一种诧异或不解的眼光看着我："你怎么会选这样一个专业啊？"除了我，还有一位同学考了个非主流专业——阿拉伯语，估计我们俩是当时那一届公认的两个怪咖吧。家里人起初听到我要学习中文也很惊讶，但是在知道我很确定之后，给了我充分的支持。我记得母亲回忆说，她那一辈人上学时，中国对英国人来讲就跟月亮差不多远！

人们一直说中国文化博大精深，这个说法一点不为过。我在中国最早去的地方是青岛：我2006年在一家双语幼儿园当幼师。后来又在海洋大学学习半年。就连现在，听到山东口音的时候会倍感亲切。后来到上海外国语大学读硕士，学习翻译。学无止境，越学越意识到自己知识是多么的有限。

就说中国地理吧，中国地方大，各地在语言、饮食与习俗上的差异是非常大的。这对我来说既是个挑战又是个诱惑；光在一个国家就可以学习好几种语言，跟很多不同的人打交道、交朋友。去唱K的话有普通话、英语、闽南语和粤语歌曲。我对各种音乐都感兴趣；从带着浓浓北京腔的"现实派"地下说唱组合阴三儿，到经典流行歌手张学友和梁静茹，再到台湾摇滚的伍佰，我都喜欢。在上海吃饭的话可以半夜吃羊肉串喝啤酒当宵夜，还可以吃陕西biangbiang面、本帮菜、粤菜点心、川菜火锅和口水鸡。

如何描述中国人？如果要说一个共同点，那就是中国人非常好客。从哈尔滨到北京，从上海到长沙，我都感受到了中国是个礼仪之邦。中国人很热情，很愿意交朋友，这我很喜欢。如果非得说点不太好听的，就是中国的地域意识很强：各个地方的人，哪怕是一个很小的地方出来的，都热爱自己的家乡。这一点我认为有个坏处，就是可能会不太喜欢"外地人"。我有时候希望中国人可以多到中国其他地方去生活、工作，多了解一下其他地方的人和事。

这几年我在上海很开心。上海是个现代化的国际大都市；同时，它还有丰富的历史。我喜欢晨跑，经常会跑到外滩那边，会路过很多老建筑。上海还有很多英国缺乏的东西——如果说一个的话，那就是密室逃脱。从比较小的、道具简单的，到豪华高档的，玩起来非常有意思。现在伦敦也有一些，但是远远没有上海的普遍。我喜欢跟朋友一起破解里面的密码与迷题，尽管自己的贡献可能比较小——心算没有中国朋友强。密室逃脱里的场景让我回想起小时候看的一个电视节目《水晶迷宫传奇》[1]。

中国的文学又离不开"博大精深"四个字。想看的书实在太多，从古代的唐传奇，到《红楼梦》这样的名著，到现代的言情、武侠小说。而自从我学习翻译以来，我更加想把中国文化的这些精彩之处介绍给我的同胞。我希望在接下来的几年可以在这个方面做出一点点贡献，也同时帮助我的学生了解到我们英国的更多文化。

作者简介：

George Fleming（费祖志，英国籍）在剑桥大学攻读汉学本科专业，毕业后来上海外国语大学读研究生口译专业。在做了三年全职翻译后开始担任上海外国语大学教师，现在高级翻译学院笔译系教汉英笔译。

1　译者注：水晶迷宫传奇（The Crystal Maze），又称水晶迷宫，是恰特沃兹电视制作公司于1990年至1995年在英国第四台（Channel 4）播出的一个益智节目，由主持人带领六名参赛者勇闯迷宫重重关卡，赢取最终大奖。

A PIECE OF KOREA IN SHANGHAI

Myung A Lee

My first encounter with China was a decade ago: I was in Beijing, learning Chinese. I couldn't speak a word at the time and the language barrier caused me considerable difficulties. South Korea and China are both part of the East Asian cultural sphere but are different in many ways. It was those small differences that sparked my curiosity and desire to explore ever further. Every time I picked up my Chinese textbook, I didn't want to put it down, even to the point of forgetting to eat or sleep. I was totally immersed in my study of Chinese. When my friends chatted with me, I would throw myself into the conversation enthusiastically.

However, time is always short. After I graduated from my course in Beijing, I hurriedly packed up my things and returned to Korea, working nine to five. I gradually grew tired of the busy pace of work and constant business trips, and my long-buried longing for China came aflame once more. Thanks to the recommendations of friends, and good fortune, I gained the chance to pursue a doctorate in Shanghai. When that happened, I resigned without a moment's hesitation and returned to China. This time, however, I was headed not for Beijing, but for Shanghai: home of the Pearl of the Orient, and the perfect fusion of traditional culture and modernity.

China is undergoing massive changes: the people are the same, but their surroundings are not. The Chinese were just as warm and welcoming as ever, but everything about the country had been transformed since my previous visit. Before I had time to really appreciate these huge changes, I was rushed into my research work. My accommodation was a fair distance from the university, which is in the downtown area, so every day I would wake up early and feel my way through the darkness. Three years went by without my noticing it. After I completed my doctorate, my teachers and Professor Jin graciously recommended me for further study, allowing me to continue at SISU doing post-doctoral research.

I have been living in Shanghai for almost four years now. I arrived knowing nothing; later on, I knew a little; and now, I know a little bit more. Over the same period, my dealings with the Chinese have transformed them from strangers to acquaintances, and then to friends. I had some difficulties while I was a student in Beijing, but now my hardships have softened. I left my country on my own, so some homesickness was inevitable. Nevertheless, this trip to China studying Chinese-Korean comparative linguistics has given me a great many more opportunities to get acquainted with the students and faculty at the Korean department, so I haven't missed home so much. Before I came to SISU, my friends were uniformly Chinese and I spoke Chinese every day. As I immersed myself gradually into life here, I began to forget some of my native etiquette and habits. Once, the university held a large event, after which I had dinner with my teachers. When it came to the toasts, one of the teachers criticized me, saying that I didn't seem Korean at all — I hadn't toasted in the unique Korean way. At that moment, I was mortified. In Korea, it is the custom that when drinking with someone older than yourself, you should turn away from them to empty your glass. I think this is a sign of my assimilation into Chinese society, which was reflected in my language, way of thinking, and habits.

After coming to the Korean department at SISU, I have put in a regular appearance at different events and mixed a lot with the students of the department. I am truly amazed by their ability. They not only speak excellent Korean, but have a deep understanding of traditional Korean culture and habits. In some sense, they are more "Korean" than the Koreans. At the ceremony to mark the 20ᵗʰ anniversary of the founding of the department, Professor Jin Jishi received an award from the university recognizing his work. After the ceremony was over, I returned to my dorm and to my own work. One day, some of my female classmates telephoned me, saying they wanted to throw a party in our supervisor's honor and asked if I had any advice. I felt really ashamed at the time. When I was a master's student in Korea, my classmates and I would often do that kind of thing for our teachers. I had forgotten so many things, all of which were so valuable. Learning is a never-ending process: it seems like I could learn a good thing or two from my younger classmates about Korean etiquette. They also reminded me of what my parents taught me when I was young: respect for one's teachers and good manners. I'm a student again.

About the author:

Myung A Lee (Korean) earned a doctorate from the Chinese faculty at East China Normal University before coming to SISU's post-doctoral research mobile unit.

上海的小韩国

李明儿（韩国）

　　我与中国的第一次接触是十年前我在北京学汉语。那时候的我一句汉语都不会说，语言上的障碍让我吃尽了苦头。虽然韩国和中国同属东方文化圈，但在许多方面还是存在着差异的，而那看似微不足道的差异激发了我的好奇心，让我不断地为之探索。每当我拿起汉语书时，总是爱不释手。我废寝忘食，沉浸于汉语之中，当周围的朋友和我聊天，我总是能兴致勃勃地跟他们侃上几句。

　　然而时光总是那么的短暂，在北京毕业之后，我匆匆打上行囊，回到了韩国，从此过上了朝九晚五的生活。忙碌的工作，永不休止的出差，让我渐渐地感到了一丝厌倦，埋在内心深处的对中国的思念之情油然而生。得益于好友的推荐以及上天的眷顾，我得到了来上海攻读博士的机会。当时我毫不犹豫地辞掉工作，重新踏上了中国之路，而这次的目的地不是北京，而是中国的东方明珠，传统文化与现代文明完美结合的上海。

　　沧海桑田，人是物非。中国人还是那样的亲切友好，而中国的一切早已发生了天翻地覆的变化。我还没来得及感慨中国的巨变，就又匆匆忙忙地投入到研究之中。由于我的宿舍离市内的校区有点距离，我每天很早起来摸黑赶路。一晃三年就过去了。我的博士课程结束后，承蒙老师的提拔以及金教授的厚爱，我进入了上海外国语大学博士后研究站研究。

我在上海生活快四年了，从当初的一无所知，到后来的一知半解，到如今的略知一二，我跟中国人沟通也经历了这样一个历程：陌生——相识——相近。在北京时碰到的一些苦头，如今转化成了甜头。虽然我只身一人，背井离乡，免不了一些思乡之苦，但这次到上海外国语大学学习中韩语言对比，跟韩语系学生和老师交流的机会倍增，思乡之情也就得到了缓解。来上外之前，我的周围清一色是中国朋友，每天使用的语言都是汉语，在熏陶渐染的同时，我慢慢地淡忘了韩国的一些礼节和习惯。有一次，学校举行了重大的活动，活动完了之后，跟老师们聚餐敬酒时，有位老师批评我说，韩国人敬酒有独特的礼节，而我不像韩国人。那时，我尴尬得无地自容。依照韩国的传统礼节，在长辈面前喝酒时，应该把身体转向侧面，避开对着长辈喝酒。我想这是我中国化的一个标志，从语言上、思想上，到文化习惯上。

到了上外韩语系，我经常会参加系里活动，跟这里的学生有了许多交流，韩语系学生的实力让我感到惊讶不已。他们不仅语言能力出众，而且深谙韩国的文化传统习惯，从某种方面来说，他们比韩国人还韩国。在韩语系建系20周年庆典上，我们金基石教授得到了学校授予的杰出贡献表彰。活动结束之后，我就又回到宿舍开始忙自己的事。有一天，师妹们打电话给我，她们想给导师开个庆祝会，来咨询我的意见。那时，我自己感到相当惭愧。在韩国读硕士时，我跟同学们照常都会那样做的。很多东西被我遗忘了，而那些东西是何其珍贵啊。学无止境，看来我这个韩国师姐要向他们好好学习韩国礼节了。师妹们也让我想起了小时候父母对我的教诲，人必须尊师敬道。我又重新上路了。

作者简介：

李明儿（韩国籍）毕业于华东师范大学中文系博士学位，现担任上海外国语大学博士后科研流动站研究员。

"PRACTICING WHAT I LEARN" IN THE SISU COMMUNITY[1]

Indira Priyadarshini Ravindran

Dear friends and colleagues, respected leaders of the university,

As I reviewed my lecture notes last night, in preparation for today's class on India-China Relations, I was struck by the fact that the earliest exchanges between these two countries were scholarly in nature. Buddhists monks and scholars trekked across the Himalayas to meet their counterparts, to learn and to share. In fact scholars and scientists from all over the world traveled to ancient China, as did merchants and explorers. They were received across several dynastic periods by various Imperial courts. China has almost always opened its doors to teachers and to

---

1 注：本文为Indira P. Ravindran女士在2014年9月上海外国语大学外国专家迎新见面会上发表的致辞。

learners alike.

As all of you know, this week's headline news is about the success of billionaire entrepreneur: Ali Baba's Jack Ma, the richest man in China. In fact, he is the *richest Chinese person* in the world. Suddenly, it occurred to me that the *most famous Chinese person* in the world is not a businessman or woman, or politician, or war hero, or a movie star. Rather, the most famous Chinese person in the world is a Teacher, a Scholar, a Philosopher, who did not possess material wealth, but only spiritual riches.

I refer of course to Kong Zi, Confucius. I quote from the opening line of the Analects:

O, how I enjoy practicing what I learn constantly!

What ecstasy that distant friends come to me!

We come from many different countries, cultures, and intellectual backgrounds. We come from distant lands. Tonight, in this beautiful campus, in this hall, all these distances have disappeared.

My name is Indira, I was born and raised in India, and I completed my postgraduate education in the US and lived there for several years. I now live and work in China. I'm honored to be here with all of you. Like you, I have had a fabulous welcome here at SISU. I have been enjoying my time with my students; my colleagues; and in the beautiful new gardens and buildings at Songjiang. It is a privilege to teach at a historical university such as Shang-Wai; to teach such bright, eager students.

There are 100 different reasons to admire Shang-Wai. However, in my opinion, the pillars of the university are the wonderful administrative & service staff and the colleagues who ensure the smooth functioning of the various departments, the libraries, and the Foreign Affairs Office. These are the people who enrich the everyday experience of the teachers and the students and I applaud them.

Dear teachers, I wish each of you great success in your classes, and outside your classes. May you enrich and be enriched by China, where teachers hold the highest respect in society.

Now I wish to share with you my China story.

In India, and especially in the United States, I have had the opportunity to interact with several multi-racial community organizations, and with activists who strive daily for social justice and equality. I have been inspired by their values, and I've always wanted to live in a Socialist country, so when my family received the opportunity to move to China, I was thrilled!

Then I landed at Pudong International airport. It did not quite correlate with the Socialist ideal I had nurtured in my mind. As our family settled in, Shanghai continued to shock my senses; China continued to rock my world. That was 7 years ago. Today, my children are native mandarin speakers. We live in a Chinese compound with Shanghainese neighbors; our "family" includes our dear helpers.

When I see the Lujiazui skyline, I see Manhattan on steroids, and I smile. It no longer shocks me. I'm just beginning to understand the meaning of Socialism with Chinese characteristics. In fact, all these theories and academic concepts come to life in unexpected and interesting ways in China. As a trained political scientist, I find myself testing and assessing these concepts all the time. To be an effective teacher, you need to be a lifelong learner. In China, the learning never ceases.

Of course there are no roses without thorns. My "China story" includes frustrating moments — almost on a daily basis, whether it's trying to convince a local Shanghainese that I do speak some mandarin, or it's trying to find vegetarian food. And then, there's the matter of the internet, which has a mind of its own: I call it "internet with Chinese characteristics"! But this is all part of the game, and you learn to take things in your stride.

So, why does this place feel like home to me? Well... What I love most is the everyday humanity; the everyday simplicity; the egalitarianism; the affection of friends; the kindness of strangers; the endless possibilities I see in the young eyes of my students...

Ladies and gentlemen, this is China.

This is the home of brilliant billionaire Jack Ma. This is the home of Kong Zi, Confucius, who did not own anything, but has left us immeasurable treasures.

I close again with the words of the great master:

If you think in terms of a year, plant a seed;

If in terms of ten years, plant trees;

If in terms of 100 years, teach the people.

Clearly, SISU is thinking in terms of the next 100 years. I wish you greater and greater success always. And I thank you for inviting me to be a part of this exciting journey. Xie Xie Da Jia!

About the author:

Indira Priyadarshini Ravindran (Indian) earned PhD in international political relations from Johns Hopkins University before teaching international relations and public affairs at SISU.

学而致用在上外

Indira Priyadarshini Ravindran（印度）

亲爱的朋友们、同事们，尊敬的校领导：

昨晚，当我为今天的中印关系课准备讲义时，这样一段事实打动了我：从本质上来看，中印两国早期的交流都是学术性的。众多佛教信徒、僧侣、学者翻越喜马拉雅山脉，去拜会同道、学习、交流。事实上，全世界的学者、科学家都到古代中国游历，商人、探险家亦是如此。历经数代，他们受到朝廷的接待。中国几乎一直向教导者、求学者敞开国门。

众所周知，本周的头条新闻是阿里巴巴富豪企业家马云的成功，他可以称得上是中国最富有的人。事实上，他也是世界上最富有的中国人。突然间，我想到：世界上最著名的中国人并非某位商人、政治家、战斗英雄或者电影明星，而是一位导师、学者、哲人，他自己并不坐拥物质财富，但拥有无尽的精神财富。

当然，我说的这个人就是孔子。引用他的《论语》开篇：

学而时习之，不亦说乎？

有朋自远方来，不亦乐乎？

我们来自众多不同的国家，有不同的文化、专业背景，我们来自遥远的地方。今晚，在这美丽的校园，在这宴会大厅里，所有距离都消失了。

我叫英迪拉，生长于印度，在美国获得研究生学位，在那里居住过几年。目前在中国生活、工作。我很荣幸与各位在此相聚。同你们一样，我在上外受到了热情的欢迎。在美丽的松江校园，与学生、同事共度的时光使我倍感喜悦。能够在像上外这样的历史名校任职，指导如此聪颖好学的学生，是我的殊荣。

上外可以有100个受到赞扬的理由。然而，在我看来，这所大学的支柱是其优秀的行政人员，他们确保各个院系、图书馆、对外合作交流处能够有效运作，他们确保全校师生的日常生活充实圆满，我感谢他们。

亲爱的老师们，我祝各位在课堂内外都获得巨大成功。教师在中国社会享有崇高地位，愿你们珍惜中国，同时也被中国珍惜。

下面我想与大家分享我的中国故事。

在印度时，尤其在美国时，我有机会接触一些由多种族人员参加的社区组织，并与当中的积极分子交流，他们整日为社会公平正义奔走奋斗。受他们的价值观影响，我一直想在社会主义国家居住，当得知能够举家迁往中国时，我异常兴奋。

我们的飞机在浦东国际机场降落。这里与我脑海中理想的社会主义不太一致。家人安顿好之后，上海的一切，持续震撼着我的心灵；中国的一切，也在持续颠覆着我的世界。但那是在7年前。今天，我的孩子可以说流利的中文，我们住的院子周围有上海邻居；我的"家庭"成员也包括了我们的家政人员。

当我远眺陆家嘴时，那似乎是曼哈顿的升级版，于是我笑了。这一切都不会再震撼到我了。我也开始明白中国特色社会主义的含义。实际上，在中国所有这些理论和学术概念都在以意想不到的有趣方式呈现出来，作为一个专业的政治学者，我发现自己一直都在测评这些概念。要想教得好，就得终身学习。在中国，学无止境。

当然，玫瑰带刺，美中不足。我的"中国故事"也有沮丧的时候，基本上天天都有，比如要上海人确信我会说一点普通话的时候，或是寻找素食的时候，还有就是互联网的问题，连它都有自己的意识——我称之为"中国特色互联网"！但情况就是这样，你要学会泰然处之。

所以，为何这里让我感到宾至如归呢？对，我最爱的是这平常的仁慈、平常的朴素；是平等、友爱、互助；是我在年轻学生眼里看到的无限可能。

女士们，先生们：这里就是中国。

这里是杰出富豪马云的故乡，也是孔子的故乡。孔子一无所有，但却留给我们无尽财富。

最后我想再次引用这位圣人的名言：

一年之计，莫如树谷；

十年之计，莫如树木；

终身之计，莫如树人。[1]

显然，上外正在谋划它的终身树人之计，祝你们成功。感谢你们邀请我加入这激动人心的旅程。谢谢大家！

作者简介：

Indira Priyadarshini Ravindran（印度籍）毕业于美国约翰·霍普金斯大学国际政治关系博士学位，现为上海外国语大学国际关系和公共事务学院教师。

---

1 译者注：此句出自《管子·权修》，非孔子言。

LEARNING CHINESE

Mickaël Muraz

I arrived in Shanghai in 2013 to teach French.

I wasn't here to learn Chinese, but from my first days here, I realized that English wasn't going to be much help in communicating with the Chinese. Thrown into this world of indecipherable symbols, I felt cut off from the rest of the world. I was illiterate.

Walking through the streets, I would meet people and exchange a look, but couldn't string two words together. I would see Chinese characters on restaurant menus, on product labels in the supermarket, or on the keypad of a washing machine, but saw only a mass of lines, curves and dots.

In French, we say something is "like Chinese" to refer to something incomprehensible. What do the Chinese say?

After a while, I was managing to get by with hand gestures. I would point at something on the menu and could top up my metro card. After a little longer, with patience, perseverance and invention, I could open a bank account, get a phone number, or borrow books from the library. Small victories.

Learning Chinese

After several months in Shanghai, I began to take Chinese lessons at a private school a stone's throw from SISU. The dialogue we practiced in the first lesson went as follows:

你好！我叫山本，是日本人。

Hello! My name is Mr. Yamamoto. I'm Japanese.

你好！我叫大卫。

Hello! I'm David.

你是法国人吗?

Are you French?

是。

Yes.

Chinese is notoriously difficult to learn due to its lack of an alphabet and its pronunciation (with four separate tones). The grammar on the other hand is relatively simple. Learning Chinese means becoming a child, writing line after line of characters in an exercise book after school to commit them to memory.

To be honest, I didn't study Chinese in order to talk to my Chinese colleagues, who spoke excellent French and often English, or to my students or other international colleagues — but for everybody else. The more I learned of the language, the more I felt I understood Chinese behavior and their way of thinking. From the point of view of a native French beginner, the Chinese language is very direct, unburdened by overly complicated polite expressions. The language you hear in the street and in the shops is straight to the point, pragmatic, and dispenses with every word that doesn't help convey the message. Unlike French, when you want the bill at a restaurant, there is no "Excuse me, would you mind bringing us the bill, please?" Instead, a simple "Bill!" does the job. Having said that, I imagine that Chinese literature, which has been passed down through the centuries, is very different, but I can't yet read it.

I speak a little Mandarin…

Shanghai is a large city, and you can get by without speaking Chinese. Many foreigners live in China for many years and continue to speak English. With a smattering or a basic grasp of the language, you can have a simple conversation with strangers and begin to feel part of the Chinese language world. Even if the road is long, even if it takes me several years to have a real conversation with the Chinese, the pleasure of learning and speaking is well worth the work.

Philosopher and writer Emil Cioran once said, "One doesn't live in a country; one lives in a language."

One day, I'd like to live in China.

When in China, foreigners are thrown into an ocean of unknown signs and symbols. It's easy to get lost. Every street corner hides an undiscovered world. A look, a cry, a gesture can catch one off guard by its tenderness or abruptness, but the experience is normally positive because these never carry a hint of aggression. They are happy accidents. In China, you have to get used to never being alone, to being constantly under observation. People fix you with a curious gaze, strange foreigner that you are, reminding you that you're different. Living in China makes me feel more alive than living anywhere else.

About the author:

Mickaël Pierre Muraz (French) graduated with a Master's degree from Université Stendhal, and now teaches French language at the School of French and Francophone Studies, SISU.

我学汉语

Mickaël Muraz（法国）

来到中国

2013年，我来到上海教授法语。

我来的初衷并非是为了学习汉语，然而从在上海的第一天起，我便意识到在中国用英语与中国人交流并不是很行得通。来到这个充斥着陌生符号的世界，我们似乎与世界隔绝了。文盲，名副其实。

走在路上，每每遇到别人，我们互相用眼神打个招呼，但却无法开口问候。看着饭店菜单上的汉字，超市商品上的标签，洗衣机上的按钮，除了直线、曲线和点，别的什么都看不明白。

在法语里，我们用"这像中国话一样"来形容一样东西令人费解，那在汉语中，你们又会怎么说呢？

过了不久，我可以指着菜单点菜，给交通卡充钱，再然后，凭借着耐心、坚持、创造力，在银行开了账户，开通了手机号，在图书馆借了书。这些都是属于我们老外的小小的胜利。

学习汉语

来这儿几个月以后，我开始在离大学不远的一家私立学校学习中文，第一课我们学了这样的对话：

——你好！我叫山本，是日本人。

——你好！我叫大卫。

——你是法国人吗？

——是。

众所周知，中文因其非字母的书写系统和四声的发音非常难学，而它的语法却相对简单。学习中文的过程就同个孩子一般，放学后在纸上一遍遍练习横竖撇捺，为了把它们牢牢记住。

说真的，我学中文并不是为了和我的中国同事交流，他们的法语都很好，英语也是。也不是为了我的学生或是外国同事，我是为了和其他人交流。在学习的过程中，我越来越能理解中国人的行为和思维模式。在我看来，作为一名初学汉语的法国人，汉语是一门直白的语言，不受繁复的客套话的阻碍。在街上，在商店里，我们听到的是一种务实的、高效的、摒弃一切无用信息的直白语言。比方说，用法语我们要说"不好意思，请问您可以把账单给我们吗？"，而在这儿，我们只用一句"买单"就够了。由此我想到中国文学，经过几个世纪的传承，是非常高深的，但我还未能窥见一斑。

我会说一点点普通话

上海是个大城市，即使不会说中文也可以生存。许多外国人在中国生活了很多年却还是说着英语。学习一些基础的中文，最基本的水平就能够让我与陌生人说话，能够感受到自己融入这个团体中，成为说汉语的一份子。哪怕路很长，哪怕要很多年的学习才能真正拥有汉语的学识，但理解和表达的乐趣却还是使这些辛苦变为值得。

萧沆（罗马尼亚旅法作家，同时也是一位哲学家）曾经说过："我们不居住在一个国度中；我们栖息在他的语言里。"

有朝一日，我想住在中国。

对外国人来说，在中国就如同沉浸在一个陌生符号和声音的海洋，很容易就迷失了。大街小巷每个角落都有不经意的未知风景。一瞥，一呼，一举止，都会让人为这里的刚和柔所倾倒，这些接触从不带任何攻击性，而是充满了正能量，因此都是美丽的意外。在这里，要学会被簇拥被打量。一双双好奇的眼睛盯着我们，异国风情的异国人，让我方才想到，我和他们不一样。我在中国，我活在中国，比任何地方更让我觉得我活着。

作者简介：

Mickaël Pierre Muraz（法国籍）毕业于格勒诺布尔司汤达大学硕士学位，于2013年9月至2015年6月期间担任上海外国语大学法语系教师。

MY CHINA STORY

Maria Luisa Tornotti

The first time I came to China was on an official visit to Beijing in 1998. At that time, foreigners knew little about China, with some unaware even of Chinese New Year. I personally had researched Chinese history and what are thought of as the classics of Chinese thought, such as *The Analects, Tao Te Ching, Chuang Tzu*, and had also touched on the *I Ching*. However, after I arrived in China, people told me nobody actually read these books because they were obscure and difficult to understand. Of course, the versions I had read before were in Italian.

In China I have come to appreciate pragmatism and poetry. I think these two have formed the Chinese character. I have noticed that many people have a love for the natural world, enjoying the beauty of every flower and tree, the burgeoning flora of spring, and the browning foliage in autumn. I have noticed people stop under the shade of a tree to rest or think.

Of course, the China I see is constantly changing. Modernization is creating ever fancier, loftier skyscrapers with more than a few luxury ones among their number. The streets are chockablock with cars. Some hazardous factories have moved out of the city and there has been an obvious improvement in people's standard of living. However, China is also a society with a large income disparity, and wealth and luxury have been placed on a pedestal. Out of the many large, luxury cars weaving through the streets of Shanghai, many only have one passenger — at the wheel. Smaller cars may be more practical, for the kids' school run, for instance, rather than a vehicle which serves as a tool to flaunt one's wealth. Everyone here is very outgoing, witty, a great talker and of course extremely hardworking and ambitious. They treat us internationals in an open and friendly way. We feel really free and at ease here. Although as everybody knows, Shanghai is a huge metropolis, it retains a strong connection to Nature. Shanghai's parks, along with the smaller tracts of similar land on university campuses, are open to the public. This is something great and really citizen-friendly. It's without a doubt absolutely necessary.

On the other hand, the difficulty for us lies in how to adapt to a completely new environment, from the diet to daily habits, all of which are in stark contrast to abroad. Still, we can keep our different lifestyles, especially in terms of diet, which is also much needed to remain in good health. Imported foods are readily available everywhere here. Although they're a bit pricey, there is a complete range of fruit and vegetables on offer. Issues of communication go without saying, but my experiences tell me to learn to be patient; those issues will be solved over time.

China's pursuit of modernization has already expanded, but this is not enough. Every nation should face its history, its past, and adapt them without fear to the pace of modernization. The process is the same for every people; it will wear down the cultural barriers between different nations and cause those countries without much history, like the UAE, to stand out, but this is not enough. Everyone may race to build the highest skyscraper, but this sort of difference is superficial. Actually, it is culture that creates the differences between different nations, and is one of the interesting things in life.

Consumerism is no substitute for values, although we can feel its dominance all around us. On the other hand, calculating materialism will pose a danger to the common values of the Chinese people. Every nation has certain currents of thought well known to its young people; these sincere ideals enrich the minds of the young, bringing fulfillment, compensating for the vacuum left by pious religious faith, and helping them to abandon their pursuit of fame and gain.

China should try and improve its international reputation. We admire China's tremendous efforts to become a global superpower, but that does not mean we agree absolutely with the idea. For instance, when I tell people that the Chinese help and protect stray cats in the parks on their own initiative, these people don't believe me because they think the Chinese still eat cats (and dogs). Unfortunately, I can't say that these people are completely wrong, because I have seen Chinese eating these animals with my own eyes. Still, I can say that there are many Chinese who care, and who appreciate the value of wildlife and Nature.

Just a few days ago, I saw something really touching. At the school next to where I live, some Chinese students discovered a chubby cat that had been gravely hurt. They called in a vet and now those students have pooled their money to foot the cat's veterinary bill. Of course, if these poor animals had a better environment, or those looking after them could show that they cared, perhaps we wouldn't have to do these things. There are actually many people working to help these animals but their kindness is often hampered by the environment. In the West we learn about respecting wildlife in our textbooks and that we are not masters of the natural world, but an inseparable part of it. Modern science has proved this in a range of different ways.

I will be happy to see more young people get involved in caring for the environment rather than caring about what clothes to wear. Apathy is a terrible thing, but it exists between different countries, and between different good-natured and welcoming nations. This apathy is like those slow-witted or numb people. Actually, there is no national barrier between souls; it's nothing to do with nationality.

About the author:

Maria Luisa Tornotti (Italian) graduated from the University of Milan and currently teaches Italian at the department of Italian, School of European and Latin American Studies, SISU.

我的中国故事

Maria Luisa Tornotti（意大利）

　　我第一次来到中国的时候是受政府派遣来到北京，那是1998年。当时外国人对中国知之甚少，甚至对中国的春节也一无所知。就我个人而言，我研究过中国的历史，阅读了被认为是承载中国传统思想的相关著作，比如《论语》、《道德经》、《庄子》，我对《易经》也有所涉猎。然而来到中国后，别人却告诉我他们并不读这些书，因为它们实在晦涩难懂。当然，我之前读的都是意大利语的版本。

　　在中国我学会了欣赏实用主义和诗歌情怀，我认为恰是这些塑造了中国人的个性。我注意到很多人对于自然世界的钟情，我看到他们满怀欣喜地欣赏一花一木的美丽，欣赏百花齐放的盛况，欣赏满目红叶的秋景，也看到他们驻足在树下休憩思考的身影。

　　当然我也看到中国的面貌在不断发生改变。现代化的推进使得高楼大厦愈加富丽、高耸，其中不乏壮丽奢华的建筑。街道上车水马龙，一些有害环境的工厂也从重要的大城市迁离，人们的生活水平得到明显改善。然而社会两极分化尤为明显，对财富及奢侈生活的崇尚显而易见。在穿梭于上海的豪华轿车中，多数只有一位司机在驾驶；或许小型汽车更为实用，比如用来接送孩子上下学，而不是将豪车作为炫耀财富的必需品。这里的人们都十分开朗、风趣、健谈，当然也勤于工作，积极向上；他们对于我们这些外国人也抱着开放和友好的态度。我们在这里感到十分自在。虽然众所周知上海是一个大都市，但是这座城市并不缺乏与自然的联系。这所城市的公园，包括大学校园里那些面积不大的花园，都欢迎着公众的来访。这一点既美好又亲民，毫无疑问也是非常有必要的。

另一方面，对于我们外国人而言，困难的地方在于如何适应一个截然不同的环境。无论是饮食还是日常习惯上，中国都与我们自己国家有很大差异，但我们可以保留这些不同的生活习惯，尤其是在饮食方面，这对身体健康也是很有必要的。如今到处都可以买到进口食品，虽然蔬菜和水果有些昂贵，但品种齐全，数量丰富。沟通交流方面的问题则不言而喻，但我的经历告诉我，我们都需要一定的时间和耐心去理解和适应。

中国对于现代化的推崇已经扩散开来，但这仍然不够。每一个民族都应该正视自己的历史和过去，并且毫无畏惧地让其适应现代化的步伐。现代化进程对于所有民族都是一样的，它会磨平我们的文化差异，让那些缺少历史的民族比如阿联酋脱颖而出，但这样是不够的。或许大家可以比赛谁建造的摩天大楼更高，但这些其实都大同小异。事实上，只有文化才能铸就每个民族的特点，而这也正是对人类而言颇有趣味的一点。

消费主义并不能取代价值观，虽然我们处处可以感受到它的统治地位。而另一方面，处心积虑汲汲营营的价值观，则会将中国人团结一致的品性置于危险之中。每一个民族在其历史长河中都有些许思想脉络是为年轻一代所熟知的，这些无比真诚的思想是为了丰富他们的内在世界，消除空虚，弥补虔诚信仰的缺失，放下对名利的追逐。

中国应当试图提升其国际声誉。我们对于中国为成为世界超级强国而做出的巨大努力抱着欣赏的态度，但这并不意味着我们对此持有完全肯定的观点。就比如当我和别人讲起有一些人自愿帮助和保护公园里的流浪猫时，他们并不相信，因为他们认为中国人仍然会以猫狗为食。遗憾的是，我无法彻底反驳他们的想法，因为我亲眼看到过这样的现象，但是我仍然可以说有很多人是怀有大爱的，他们珍视动物和大自然。

就在几天前我亲眼见证了令我非常欣慰的一幕。在我家旁边的学校里，几个中国学生发现了一只伤得很重的肥猫，他们找来了一位兽医，现在他们一起负担这只猫在兽医院的治疗费用。当然，如果这些可怜的动物有一个更好的生存环境，照顾它们的人能给予一些爱心，或许我们就不需要做这些了。确实有些人在努力帮助这些动物，但他们的善举常常受环境阻碍。事实上，我们西方人从西方文化的教科书中学到的是对动物的尊重，我们并不是自然的主人，而是其中不可分割的一部分。而现代科学已经从不同角度证实了这些观念。

我会很高兴看到更多的年轻人投入到保护大自然中，而不是过于追求穿着打扮。漠不关心是一件很糟糕的事，但这种冷漠仍然存在于不同国家之间，也存在于那些拥有善良心地以及开放心胸的民族之间；冷漠正如那些迟钝而麻木的人一样。事实上在不同民族的灵魂之间是不存在国别障碍的，这些是不分国界的。

作者简介：

Maria Luisa Tornotti（意大利籍）毕业于米兰大学，现担任上海外国语大学西方语学院意大利语系教师。

四、感悟篇

OBSERVATIONS OF CHINA: SOME THOUGHTS

Choi Choon Heum

I have learned a lot from my experiences in China. I first began to want to understand the country when I was at university — and that desire is the reason why I eventually became the researcher of China's international relations I am today. Shanghai International Studies University gave me the opportunity to become one of their faculty members, teaching Chinese students, which has given me a front-line insight into everything that is happening in China at the moment.

Over the past 25 years, my learning and cooperation with the Chinese has showed me, and let me hear and understand many things. Even my way of thinking has become more Chinese. This is what I had hoped for. To make up for gaps in my knowledge, I not only studied Chinese culture, history and how the Chinese view the future, I have also gained a lot by talking to the Chinese themselves. Specifically, my observations of China are as follows.

Firstly, I believe historical research is taken very seriously in China. The Chinese like to learn from their history and use the lessons of the past to help resolve the issues of the present day. Instead of completely negating, or evading, the past, I think a more beneficial approach is to correctly analyze and understand it, and then use it to solve current issues. Unless we understand the past, how can we plan for the future?

Secondly, I think China is contributing to future social and cultural development through a combination of adaptability and innovation. The former refers to the ability to adjust policy while respecting the rules. Lack of respect for the rules in favor of cutting corners and finding workarounds is merely a sort of off-the-cuff adaptation. However, what I have seen in China is development without breaking the rules, while fully tapping the potential of adaptability to improve conditions. What amazes and impresses me is that this code of conduct has become a common trait of the Chinese. They not only know how to adapt to different circumstances, but understand the value of innovation. The problem is that innovation is not something that can happen overnight; it requires constant effort, the will to continue unafraid of failure, and the patience to wait for a result. It is precisely this sort of persevering patience that has led to amazing creativity in the Chinese. As I see it, China now values the development of science and technology, and encourages application of the humanities and social sciences, thus fostering more potential for innovation. I believe China is endeavoring to promote creative thinking. Although there is a certain amount of negative publicity about China's "many counterfeit and fake products", compared to a decade ago, there are far fewer of these products in the country. Also, counterfeiting is an issue in any country. It is precisely due to China's emphasis on fostering creativity that counterfeiting is on the decline.

Thirdly, the Chinese have a very strong sense of time, interpersonal relations, and waiting. These often come to the surface in their tolerance for others. If you want to make friends in China, you need to make sure you pay attention to these three areas and learn from the Chinese in this respect. Some foreigners criticize the Chinese for their apathy to anything not directly concerning them, but I don't think of it as apathy. I believe the Chinese are simply unwilling to interfere carelessly in or express concern for a situation they do not fully understand. Sometimes I think cool detachment is a better approach to life than such careless interference.

Finally, I often see how practical the Chinese are. For instance, when they are buying vegetables, meat or fruit, they judge the quality of an item to calculate a unit price, and then figure out a total price based on the quantity. In the past I could not decide whether this was some kind of amazing consumer strategy or whether it was some form of pragmatism, because in Korea even if apples are of a different weight, the final price is still decided solely on their quality. Before, I thought it was some means of saving money, but now I think it's a sign of Chinese pragmatism, because the consumers evaluate the product from two perspectives at once (quantity and quality).

I believe that with its respect for history, ability to adapt, innovative spirit, tolerance and pragmatism, China will take a leading and significant role in the development of a more integrated Asia in the future. I have always believed this and look forward to that day.

About the author:

Prof. Choi Choon Heum (Korean) worked as senior research fellow and professor at the Korea Institute for National Unification, specializing in international relations and international and regional issues.

中国观察：我的一些思考

崔春钦（韩国）

在中国的经历使我受益良多。早在大学时期我就萌生了想要了解中国的愿望，而正是因为追随这个愿望，如今的我成为了一名研究有关中国国际关系的学者。上海外国语大学给予了我担任该校外国专家并教授中国学生的机会，使得我更加能够亲身感受发生在中国的一切。

在过去的25年里，我通过与中国的交流合作，不仅看到、听到、理解到了很多事物，就连自己的思考方式也变得和中国人更为相似。这正是我所期望的。为了弥补我知识上的不足，我不仅仅学习中国文化、中国历史以及中国人面向未来的思考方式，更通过和中国人的交流而获益。我对中国的观察具体有以下一些内容。

首先，我认为中国十分重视对历史的研究，中国人往往以史为鉴，将其应用到解决现实问题的过程中。我认为与其完全否定历史，抑或回避历史，不如正确地分析和理解历史并将其运用到现实问题上，这将会带来更多的益处。如果不知道过去，又如何去计划未来？

其次，我认为中国致力于通过灵活变通和创新精神的融会贯通来促进未来社会和文化的建设。灵活变通是指在遵守规则的前提下，根据情况的变化而调整对策。不遵守基本规则，只注重灵活变通的行为，不过是一种临机应变的策略。但是据我在中国所看的情况是，中国人在不破坏原则的前提下，充分发挥灵活性，改善不利的条件，使它向着更好的方向发展。让我觉得惊讶并感叹的是这种行为模式已成为中国人普遍拥有的一种特质。中国人不仅仅注重灵活变通，他们同样很重视创新精神，然而创新精神并不是一朝一夕就能养成的，它需要不断的努力、不畏惧失败的意志力以及耐心等待结果的思维。正是中国人的这种持之以恒的耐力才带来了惊人的创造力。在我看来，如今的中国在重视科学技术发展的同时，也鼓励其在人文社会科学领域的运用，因而能够为创新精神的培养提供更多的发展空间。我认为中国正在大力提倡创意思维的发展。虽然有一些关于中国"仿冒品和假货很多"的负面言论，但是相比十年前，这些东西在中国已经减少很多，且这种现象在任何国家都是有的。正因为中国如此的重视创新精神的培养，才使得这些现象在逐渐地减少。

第三，我发现中国人十分重视时间、人际关系和耐心等待这三个概念，这常常体现在他们宽容的性格上。所以如果你想和中国人做朋友，就需要非常重视这三方面的因素，学习中国人的宽容。有些外国人批评中国人对和自己无关的事情表现得很冷漠，但是我不认为这是一种冷漠的表现，我认为他们只是在自己不了解情况的情况下，不提倡随意干涉或者表现出他们的关心。有的时候比起随意干涉或者表现关心，淡然处之不啻于更好的处世之道。

第四，我在中国人身上常常能看到他们强调实用性的特质。例如，在买蔬菜、肉类或者水果的时候，他们首先是依据商品的质量来划定单价，再根据数量的多少来确定最终的价格。之前我一直不能断定这到底是一种惊人的商业策略还是一种实用性特质的体现，因为在韩国就算苹果的重量不一样，也是仅仅根据它的商品质量来定最后的价格。我以前觉得它是一种省钱的手段，现在更觉得这是中国人讲究实用性特质的体现，因为商品的购买者是从数量和质量两方面来同时做出评价的。

我认为，中国在具备了尊重历史、拥有灵活变通性、创新精神、宽容和实用性这五个特质的基础上，在未来亚洲共同体的建设中将发挥出重大的主导力量。对于这一点，我始终相信并且期待着。

作者简介：

崔春钦教授（韩国籍）原为韩国国家统一研究所高级研究员、教授，研究领域为国际关系学及国际区域问题研究等。

THE GARDEN

Jeroen van de Weijer

Surely the epitome of China is the public park. This is where the very young and the very old go. This is where we find the dancers, the gymnasts, the walkers (both forward and backward), an occasional jogger, the clappers, the swordsmen and the stick fighters, the birdmen and the dog people, the teachers, the chess and go players, the sick, the rich and the poor. All walks of life come together in the park, to enjoy a breath of relatively fresh air, to exercise, to catch a few extra rays of sun, just to pass some time, and, especially, to chat. The garden is never quiet.

In the garden there is harmony. Everyone leads by example, and even the dancers do not bump into each other. Discussions are loud but conflict is avoided. Children are admonished not to take toys, apples, bananas, bottles, balls, cars, and candy from their younger (or older) "brothers and sisters", and to let them watch, ride, eat, or go first. Hopes for the future are high.

In the garden everyone fulfils their designated role. Sometimes it seems that in China everyone does exactly the work they were intended to do: the gardeners are exactly right for their job, skilled workmen who turn up every day to cut the grass, trim the branches, pull out the weeds, water the plants, mostly with a smile. In a similar way the right people are in the right jobs whether they are vegetable sellers, street sweepers, office workers or watchmakers. It forces one to reflect on one's own role.

I would surely not like to miss my daily walk in the park. Apart from short but useful Chinese lessons it gives a great feeling of balance.

About the author:

Jeroen van de Weijer (Dutch) specializes in the field of linguistics. He is now a professor and doctoral supervisor from the School of English Studies, SISU.

中国的公园

耶鲁安（荷兰）

毫无疑问，中国的缩影就在它的公园。这里是大家不论长幼都会光顾的地方。在这里，你可以看到跳舞的人、做操的人、散步的人（向前散步和倒退散步的人都有）、偶尔出现的慢跑的人、拍手健身的人、练剑的人以及耍木棍的人、养鸟的人、遛狗的人、教练、下象棋和下围棋的人、养病的人、富人和穷人。社会各界的人都汇聚于此，呼吸公园中稍显新鲜的空气，锻炼身体，沐浴阳光，消磨时光。最重要的是聊天。公园里从不寂静。

在公园里，你能找到和谐。每个人都以身作则，甚至连跳舞的人都不会撞到其他人。人们扯着大嗓门聊天，但总会注意避免冲突。孩子们被警示不许拿其他"兄弟姐妹"（不论是比他们年幼或年长的孩子）的玩具、苹果、香蕉、瓶子、球类、小汽车以及糖果，他们被要求让其他同伴先看、先骑小车、先吃东西或先玩。人们对于下一代的期待总是很高的。

在公园里，每个人都很好地履行着自己的职责。有时你会觉得，每个中国人都在正确地做他们应该做的事。对于园艺师来说，这是最适合他们的工作；熟练工每天剪草、修剪树枝、拔除野草、给植物灌溉。大多数情况下，他们都笑眯眯地做这一切。类似这样各司其职的人有很多，不管是卖菜的商贩、环卫工人、办公室白领，还是钟表匠。这不禁迫使我们反思自己的角色。

我决不会错过每日在公园散步的机会。它除了给我以上这些简短却实用的思考外，还使我感受到一种很好的平衡。

作者简介：

Jeroen van de Weijer（耶鲁安，荷兰籍）为知名语言学专家，现为上海外国语大学英语学院全职教授、博士生导师。

AN UNEXPECTED ASSIGNMENT

Jonathan Huw Lumb

Nobody looks forward to the last day of their holiday. After many a glorious day spent sampling local delicacies, bathing in the sea and soaking up the sun in exotic locations, you finally have to pack up your bags, check out of the hotel and brace yourself for the journey home, during which you have ample time to think about your overflowing email inbox and the stack of work that awaits you back at the office.

Therefore, at the conclusion of a week-long trip to the Philippines with my partner in June this year, I assumed that the last day would be both tedious and unremarkable. The return leg of our flight was scheduled in the early afternoon that day, leaving us enough time for a lie-in that morning, but not enough to go out and explore the city of Puerto Princesa, where we were staying. In the end, we decided to while away the morning hours enjoying a leisurely breakfast out in the sun, while putting off the dreaded task of packing for as long as was feasibly possible.

So far, so unremarkable. It didn't take long, however, for events to take a surprising turn. Shortly after having breakfast, we were approached by a guest from an adjacent table, who complimented me on my fluent Mandarin, having overheard me chatting with my partner. It turned out that he was a newspaper columnist based in Beijing, who wrote for a major international publication. He had come to Puerto Princesa to cover the trial of a group of Chinese fishermen who had been detained by Philippine authorities after being accused of poaching endangered turtles in South China Sea. However, the trial had been postponed, so he had instead decided to try and interview the captain at the local jail in Puerto

Princesa, where the entire crew was being detained.

Despite having lived in Beijing for a number of years, this columnist did not speak good enough Mandarin to converse with the Chinese fishermen himself and needed someone to help him translate. Having overheard me speaking Mandarin at breakfast, he asked if I would be willing to assist him with his prison visit. He was in luck — not only had he found a fluent Mandarin speaker, but a Mandarin speaker who had been professionally trained as a conference interpreter. It was certainly a coincidence! Although I was keen to take on this unlikely assignment, it seemed that time wasn't on my side. Already, it was late in the morning and I needed to pack and check out of the hotel by noon to catch my early afternoon flight back to Manila. Reason would have it that I decline the request politely, return to my room and continue what had been an uneventful morning before I was interrupted. However, it seemed that curiosity got the better of me and I agreed to at least accompany this reporter as far as the local prison. It was clear from the outset, however, that we would have much to do in very little time — in just two hours, we would have to travel to the prison, negotiate our way in, conduct an interview with the detained captain and then race back to the hotel. It was already becoming apparent that this day was going to be anything but tedious and unremarkable.

After a mad drive in a tuk-tuk through rush-hour traffic, we arrived at the gates of the municipal prison in Puerto Princesa. It was a low-slung concrete building which could easily be mistaken for an old school if it wasn't for the razor wire and security guards which circled its perimeter. It was certainly an unlikely setting for the latest chapter in an ongoing maritime dispute between China and the Philippines. Having arrived at the prison, the next challenge was to find a way in, although this seemed like a bad idea at the time. To begin with, it seemed that our adventure would be over before it even began. We were told that the governor was not present and that it would be better if we came back another day. Luckily, this seasoned journalist was wise to such stalling tactics and a quick phone call to the right person was enough to secure us entry into the perimeter.

Once inside, we were again told to wait and we began to suspect that this was yet another stalling tactic to delay our interview. We were therefore slightly surprised when just ten minutes later, a Chinese individual wearing a yellow T-shirt and blue cotton shorts was escorted into the office with no introduction or fanfare. It took me a moment or two to realize that this was the captain of the Chinese fishing vessel that had been so widely reported in the media.

Given that time was limited, the columnist promptly began his interview with the captain and I did my best to interpret their dialogue. The captain of the fishing vessel seemed quite a timid man, who spoke Mandarin with a thick Hainan accent — at times, it required considerable concentration on my part to make sense of what he was saying.

It turned out that the captain and his crew had been held in detention for roughly two months and were housed in separate quarters to Filipino inmates in order to avoid any tensions. Their main enemy was boredom, with nothing to do during the many long hours they spent confined in their cells. Their jailers had tried to compensate by buying a volleyball kit for them to play with in a courtyard. However, after leaving dirty marks on some of the prison's walls, the fishermen were soon stripped of this new privilege.

Much of the interview consisted of mundane details like those in the previous paragraph. Personally, I suspect this was because the captain was unwilling to talk about the legal details of his case, given the politically charged circumstances of his arrest. In any case, we eventually ran out of time and had to curtail the interview. Thankfully, I did catch my flight back to Manila on time in the end.

Being an interpreter isn't always the most satisfying job: not every day can be exciting; not every assignment can be memorable. Like any profession, there is also a lot of routine. However, we live for those days where, like in the example above, we have the chance to meet interesting people, to witness important events and to participate in the making of history, however significant or insignificant. It is on occasions like these, where we play a pivotal role, and where other people truly depend on us, that we are reminded that the many years we spent training as an interpreter and learning foreign languages were worth all the effort after all.

About the author:

Jonathan Huw Lumb (British) obtained double honors bachelor's degree on Chinese / French at the University of Leeds in 2012 and graduated from SISU with a master's degree in English Translation and Interpretation before serving as a lecturer at the Graduate Institute of Interpretation and Translation, SISU.

意外之旅

Jonathan Huw Lumb（英国）

　　每逢假期结束，心中总有不舍。在享尽当地美食、碧海蓝天、阳光沙滩之后，人总要面对收拾行李、离开酒店、鼓足勇气迎接回家的旅途。而路上难免会想起堆积如山的邮件和办公室里待办的工作。

今年六月，当我和我的同伴即将结束在菲律宾的一周假期时，我本以为最后一天会在平淡中度过。我们回程的飞机在当天下午，足够我们睡个懒觉，但却来不及游览公主港。因此，我们决定在旅馆的露天餐厅里悠闲地吃一顿早饭借以消磨时光，同时尽量把无趣的打包任务往后拖延。

一上午都波澜不惊，但很快事情就发生了有趣的转折。饭后离席时，邻桌一个听到我们聊天的客人跟了上来，夸赞我的汉语说得很流利。原来，他是某报社驻北京的专栏作家，正在为一家知名国际出版社写稿。他此行来公主港，是想报道菲律宾当局对一批中国籍渔民的庭审。这群目前被菲律宾当局拘留的中国渔民被指控在中国南海非法捕捞某种濒危海龟。但这场庭审被延期了，所以该记者准备去采访涉案船长。船长和其他渔民都被关押在公主港的监狱。

尽管这位记者已在北京生活多年，但他的汉语还不够好，无法与那些中国渔民交流，所以他需要找个翻译。当他偶然间听到我讲中文后，便前来请我帮他进行此次采访。他很幸运，他遇到了我——不仅汉语流利，而且还受过专业的同声传译训练。实在太巧了！尽管我对此行甚感兴趣，但无奈时间不够。那时已近中午，但我尚未打包行李退房，做好准备登上下午回马尼拉的飞机。按理说，我本应婉拒这个邀约，继续我波澜不惊的一天。但我的好奇心还是占了上风，最终，我答应陪这位记者去当地监狱采访。乍看起来，我们在接下来短短的两小时内有很多事情要做——我们需要赶赴监狱，想办法进去，采访被拘留的船长，然后飞奔回酒店。显然，这一天注定不会枯燥无趣了。

当我们的出租车一路疯狂行驶过交通早高峰后，我们抵达了公主港的市政府监狱门口。那是一栋低矮的混凝土建筑，如果不是环绕四周的电网和警卫，看上去就像一所设施陈旧的学校。很难将这样一个不起眼的地方和近期闹得沸沸扬扬的中非海域争端联系起来。此时，我们先得想办法进去，尽管这看上去并不容易。难道我们的行程还未开始就要结束？门口警卫告知我们狱长那天不在，让我们改天再来。好在那位记者应对这种拖延战术非常老练，及时给某位重要人物通了个电话。最后我们被允许进入监狱。

刚一进门，我们又被告知需要等待。我们开始怀疑这是对方的又一个用以拖延采访的缓兵之计。但就在10分钟后，一个身穿黄色T恤和蓝色短裤的中国人被警卫一言不发地护送过来了。我们都对此略感惊讶。过了一会儿，我才反应过来，原来这个人就是最近被媒体广泛报道的中国船长。

因为时间有限，该记者迅速开始了对船长的采访，而我则尽力帮他们翻译。这位船长看起来很腼腆，他的普通话带着浓厚的海南口音，这需要我全神贯注去理解他的意思。

原来，船长和船员们已经被拘留了近两个月，他们和其他菲律宾囚犯是被分开关押的，以免引发冲突。在这里，这些中国船员最大的挑战是监狱生活的枯燥无聊。长时间地被关押在牢里，他们无事可做。监狱为他们买了个排球网安装在院子里，让他们消磨时间。可惜，打排球弄脏了围墙，所以他们这项新的特权又很快被剥夺了。

大部分的采访内容就像我上段描述的那样，充满了琐碎的细节。我感到，这个船长出于政治因素，不太愿意谈论这个案子的法律细节。不管怎样，我们的时间到了，不得不中止采访。谢天谢地，我当天仍然成功赶上了飞回马尼拉的航班。

做一个口译员并非世上最令人羡慕的工作，因为不是每一天都能令人激动。就像其他从业者一样，我们有大量的事务性工作。然而，就像上面的例子所说明的那样，我们得以有机会接触一些不寻常的人，见证重大的事件，甚至是参与历史的进程，不论这些历史时刻是否重要。在这样的场合，我们扮演着至关重要的角色，被客户全心依靠信赖。这时刻提醒着我们，过去多年来花在翻译训练和钻研外语上的时间是有价值有意义的。

作者简介：

Jonathan Huw Lumb（英国籍）于英国利兹大学获得汉语/法语荣誉双学士学位，2012年毕业于上海外国语大学汉英翻译口译硕士学位，现担任上海外国语大学高级翻译学院口译教师。

MY CHINA STORY

Tsukasa Kodama

I will never forget the moment I first set foot in mainland China: July 7th, 2011. I was headed for Lüshun District, Dalian, because there was someone there I absolutely had to see. That was the whole reason I had bought myself an air ticket to China. But the person I was going to meet was not Chinese; at that point we hadn't ever met. We had been pen friends since 2005, during which time over 600 letters had passed between us. We had an excellent understanding of each other's interests and plans for the future. Our correspondence had given me an impression of an intelligent and witty character; even among native Francophones, his grasp of language was among the best.

I therefore had a strong desire to travel to China, but not because of anything to do with learning Chinese. I wanted to meet this Frenchman. I still remember the first thing I ate after I arrived in Dalian: the man who was to become my husband recommended some Chinese biscuits. I accepted them, but he seemed aware of my hesitation and told me, "Don't worry. These are really good. Just pretend you don't know and enjoy them."

I have to say, compared to the confectionary friends had brought back from China in the 90s, this was something completely different. Over the subsequent twenty years, China had modernized fully and become a major economic powerhouse. At the same time, the country had become the source of many delicious biscuits, bread and cakes. When I first arrived in Lüshun, the streets were lined with shopping malls and McDonald's, and my husband was able to listen to many overseas radio stations at home. My idea of China previously had been of a place where during the peak of the harvest season, there would be power cuts throughout the cities, and where even the lifts in hotels would stop working. That trip however taught me thoroughly that my impression was out of date. What was really interesting was, as we took the taxi away from Lüshun's ever-developing city centre, the farmers and fields of the past remained, with pockets of lush green. China's environmental issues are a cause for concern, but at the time I felt that ordinary people living in Lüshun were just like people in Japan: they seemed to have no desire to completely tame Nature.

From that moment onwards, my fate was inextricable from China. I was generously embraced by the country and its open-minded people. My husband, who had lived in China for a decade when I met him, also benefitted from the welcoming nature of its people who are so easy to get on with. Even if our Chinese was slow to make progress, people would patiently speak Chinese to us or communicate with body language.

We also met many Chinese who were proficient in foreign languages. Without their many forms of help in many different languages, we would never have been able to stick it out here. Particularly when my husband was taken ill, his colleagues took great care of him. Were it not for their support, we would never have made it through that first crisis of our life together.

Now, both of us teach our native languages (French for him, Japanese for me). What sort of China will our students who study these languages and culture, hoping to give more possibilities, create in the future? I want to play a part in the education of young Chinese. By so doing, I hope I can in some small way repay China and its people for welcoming us with open arms.

About the author:

Tsukasa Kodama graduated with a Master's degree from Université Paris 8, and teaches at the School for Japanese Studies, SISU, from September 2014 to June 2015.

我的中国体验

小玉司（日本）

我永远也不会忘记第一次踏足中国大陆是在2011年7月7日。我的目的地是大连市旅顺区，那里有一个我一定要见的人，因此机缘，我买了前往中国的机票。不过住在大连的那个人并不是中国人，实际上那时我们连面都从未见过。我们从2005年开始书信往来，已经写了600多封信件，对对方的兴趣和将来的打算都了然于心。通过书信间的往来，我对他的印象是既理智又风趣，即使在以法语为母语的人中也算得上语言运用的佼佼者。

因此，我虽然憧憬中国，但来到中国的原因却并非是受汉语的吸引，而是想见见那个法国男子。我仍记得自己到大连后吃的第一口食物是现在已成为我丈夫的那个男人推荐的中国饼干。当时，虽然我收下了那块饼干，但他似乎觉察到了我的犹豫，向我说道："别担心，中国饼干可好吃了，你就当是蒙在鼓里试着吃吃看嘛。"

的确，和1990年代我吃到的通过熟人从中国带回来的点心相比，这块中国饼干已经完全不一样了。二十多年的岁月使中国完成了现代化并跻身为经济大国，同时也让她摇身变成出产美味饼干、面包以及蛋糕的国家。在我最初到访旅顺的时候，街上随处可见大商场和麦当劳，我那法国丈夫所住的宿舍还能收到好几家外国电台。之前我对中国的印象是一到丰收时节城里就会断电，连酒店的电梯都会停止运行。但是通过这次旅行，我切切实实感受到我的这种印象已经过时了。很有意思的是，当我们乘坐出租车从旅顺不断被开发的中心地带开往稍偏远的地方时，会发现昔日的农家和农田还残留着，片片绿色颇为葱郁。虽然中国的环境问题令人不安，但我当时觉得，住在这里的普通人和日本民众一样，心底丝毫没有要完全征服自然的想法。

我就这样开始了与中国的不解之缘，这个国家以及她的人民用大度的襟怀温柔地将我包容。我的丈夫能在这里生活10年以上，也是因为这个国家的人们胸襟广阔，相处起来令人舒心。即使我们的汉语总不见长进，中国人仍然不厌其烦地用汉语和肢体语言与我们交流。此外，我们还遇见了许多能将外语运用自如的中国人。如果不是他们通过各种语言对我们进行各式各样帮助的话，我们也不可能在这个地方生活下去。特别是去年我丈夫病倒的时候，他的同事给了他不少照顾。那个时候如果没有他们的支持，我们是无论如何也没法渡过这结婚以来第一场大难的。

现在，我们夫妇俩从事着各自的母语教育（丈夫教法语，我教日语）。那些通过学习我们国家的语言与文化来开拓中国未来的年轻人会创造出一个什么样的中国呢？我想为中国年轻人的教育做贡献，哪怕微不足道，也希望以此报答敞开怀抱接纳我们的中国以及中国的同志良友们。

作者简介：

小玉司（日本籍）毕业于法国巴黎八大硕士学位，于2014年9月至2015年6月期间担任上海外国语大学日本文化经济学院教师。

A BUSTLING CITY WITH ITS OWN TUNE

Ami Yamagashi

In September 2014, when I landed on the runway in Shanghai, I was immediately drawn to a sort of music. I'm not talking about strings or woodwind, or singing, but a cacophony. The noise entered my ears like a kind of music and overwhelmed my senses. For me, China — although I'm familiar only with Shanghai — is a city full of sounds.

Walk down Shanghai's streets and you will hear all sorts of sounds. First, there are people talking — and they speak very loudly. When I first came to Shanghai, I thought the people around me were having an argument and had quite a shock! (Actually, sometimes they *were* arguing about something. It was only after I had studied Chinese that I realized one naturally raises one's voice in the language.)

It's not just out in the street that people speak loudly either: people chat vigorously at the supermarket, on the bus and on the metro. Although sometimes it's a bit annoying, you can really feel the energy of life here. For someone like me who has been forbidden from speaking loudly since childhood, I envy them.

The Shanghainese often chat with strangers, like other people in the queue at the shop, or the person sitting next to them on the bus. They talk and laugh together like old friends, complaining about this or that, with an attendant rise in the supermarket or bus cacophony.

Then there are the car horns. In Japan, sounding one's horn is only permitted in an emergency; every time I hear someone press their horn I have a start. In Shanghai on the other hand, the blaring of horns is totally normal. I'm getting used to falling asleep at night in the Foreign Experts Building to the sound of car horns in the distance. The sound has already become a very familiar tune in my life.

Japan seems quiet by comparison — so much so that it seems to lack some of the life of China. No matter whether we're happy, sad, or angry, nobody can express those feelings loudly out in public, and we don't strike up conversations with strangers. People don't blare their car horns; the only sound on the roads is that of HEVs passing quietly by.

Shanghai, then, is full of a sort of noisy music. After three months living here, I have slowly come to love this music, and to begin to feel that it's perhaps better than peace and quiet — there's more vitality.

About the author:

Ami Yamagashi (Japanese) graduated with a Master's degree in Japanese Language and Education from Tokyo University of Foreign Studies, and now teaches at the School of Japanese Studies, SISU.

鸣奏喧嚣之乐的城市

山岸爱美（日本）

2014年的9月，当我走出机舱踏入上海的大地时，立刻被一种音乐吸引。这音乐既非管弦乐，亦非歌声，而是喧嚣。喧嚣之声如同音乐传入耳中，霸占了我的感官。对我而言，中国——虽然我只熟悉上海——是一座充满了声音的城市。

走在上海的街道上就会听到各种各样的声音。首先是说话声，人们说话的嗓门很大。初来上海的时候，我以为路边对话的人在吵架，还吓了一跳（其实也有吵架的时候）。学了汉语才明白，说汉语时会自然而然地提高嗓门。

说话声并非只是在路边才会那么大，超市、公交车以及地铁中人们也高声阔谈。虽说有些吵闹令人不快，但一方面又让人感受到生活的力度。我从孩提时起就被禁止大声说话，因而也会羡慕这些人。

此外，上海人也常和素不相识的人说话，比如付钱时排队的人、公交车上邻座的人等。他们如同老熟人一样谈笑，互相发牢骚，如此一来，超市和公交车上的喧嚣之乐便加大了音量。

其次是汽车的鸣笛声。在日本，只有在发生紧急情况的时候才可以鸣笛。因此，每次身边响起喇叭声我都会吓一跳。但在上海，汽车鸣笛是家常便饭。我现在逐渐习惯了在外国专家楼房间里远远听着鸣笛声入睡。鸣笛声已经成了一首我生活中十分耳熟的音乐。

这样看来，日本的城市倒是非常安静，安静得让人觉得少了些生气。人们无论高兴、悲伤还是恼怒，都不得在路边的公共场所大声表达，也不会和陌生人搭话。汽车不会鸣笛，只有油电混合车静默地驶过的声音。

相比之下，上海则充盈着名为喧嚣的音乐。在上海生活了三个月，我渐渐爱上了这首音乐。也开始觉得，似乎比起寂静，有人情味更好啊。

作者简介：

山岸爱美（日本籍）毕业于东京外国语大学日语教育学硕士学位，现担任上海外国语大学日本文化经济学院教师。

MY CHINESE STORY

Sawada Yoriko

My students often ask me: "Ms. Sawada, what brought you to China?" My answer is usually, "Because I want to do my bit to improve relations between our two countries. That's why I came to China."

I graduated from Soka University, Hachioji, Tokyo. The university, which was founded in 1971, is a relatively new, private institution. Daisaku Ikeda, the founder of Soka Gakkai, has done much to bring China and Japan closer together and holds honorary titles from many universities and institutions of higher learning in China. In December 2002, SISU became one of these, bestowing on him the title of "Honorary Professor."

Mr. Ikeda drew on his older brothers' experiences in the war to teach people about the cruelty and tragedy of war, both of which were elaborated on in his work *The Human Revolution* (1965). He has consistently said that "Japan owes China a debt of gratitude; in future, Japan must treat China well and with sincerity." In the spirit of my mentor, I came to China seeking to further the friendship between our countries. That was in 2000; the fifteen years since then have flown by.

Currently, I teach Japanese at the School of Japanese Studies, SISU. In class, I often stand next to my students, listening to their Japanese pronunciation. I pay attention to their needs and interests. I have always felt that if students like doing something, they should be encouraged to do so freely.

The "Onigiri (Rice Ball) Meeting" has long since become a tradition of our School; this year was our fourteenth. I have been involved since the inaugural event and have never missed it. Besides this, we have held 8 speaking contests and 14 debating contests, both of which are the result of my suggestions. Three years ago, the the School of Japanese Studies held a symposium attended by the different Shanghai universities on Japanese speaking and teaching methods, which saw teachers from China and Japan exchange ideas on teaching.

I have been teaching Japanese at SISU for 13 years and have taught over a thousand students to date. There is a Chinese saying that compares a teacher's students being spread all over the world, like the peaches from one tree. This is the case with me, for which I am truly happy.

As everybody knows, learning Chinese means not only learning the language but also the country's culture, habits and customs. Of course, there are many opportunities for exchange of ideas with China.

Of the students I have taught, many have helped to build bridges between China and Japan, and have made outstanding contributions to strengthening the friendship between our two nations.

It is true that at the political level, relations oscillate between warm and cold, with the occasional friction. There is a certain instability, but I am confident that people-to-people exchanges between our nations will not cool; they will grow like a steady trickle of water, with wave after wave of progress.

Two summers ago, I became seriously ill and was hospitalized and treated in Shanghai. Fortunately, I recovered and survived. That was when I made a vow to work even harder for my students and for the friendship between China and Japan.

Everyone has their own vocation in life. Why did I come to China? My aspiration to be the bridge that connects our nations has never changed.

This is my fifteenth year living in Shanghai. I want to go back to where it all began, with realizing my original ideal.

About the author:

Ms. Sawada Yoriko (Japanese) graduated from Soka University, Tokyo, and currently teaches at the School of Japanese Studies at SISU.

我的中国故事

泽田依子（日本）

　　我的学生经常问我："泽田老师，您为什么来中国呢？"这个时候我会回答："因为想为中日友好尽一份力，想成为中国与日本的桥梁，所以我来中国。"

　　我毕业于东京八王子市的创价大学。创价大学创立于1971年，是一所比较新的私立大学。创始人池田大作老师为中日友好做了很大的贡献，被许多中国的大学和机构授予了荣誉称号。2002年12月上海外国语大学也授予了他"名誉教授"的称号。

池田老师通过兄长的战争体验告诉我们"战争的残酷"和"战争的悲惨"。这在池田老师的著作《人间革命》（1965）中也很明确。老师始终呼吁"中国对日本有大恩，今后要对中国诚心诚意"。承恩师之志，我抱着为中日友好做贡献的想法来到了中国。那时正是2000年，此后15年的岁月就这样匆匆流过。

现在，我在上海外国语大学日本文化经济学院教授日语。课堂上，我常常站在学生旁边，一边倾听他们的声音一边授课，我会关注他们需要什么，对什么感兴趣。我始终觉得，如果是学生高兴做的事，就应该让他们放手去做。

"饭团大会"到现在已经成为了我们学院的传统活动，今年我们迎来了第14届。我从第一届开始每年都参加，从未缺席。此外，由我提议的"会话大会"和辩论赛也分别举办了8届和14届。三年前，这里设立了上海市大学日语会话教学方法研究会，中国教师和日本教师携手一同开展教学方法的研究活动。

我在上外已从事了13年的日语教学，至今我教过的学生已超过千人。汉语有句话叫"桃李满天下"。我在各地都有自己的学生，这让我由衷地感到欣慰。

众所周知，学习中文并非只是学习语言，还要学习中国的文化、习惯、风俗等语言以外的知识。当然，与中国交流的机会也有很多。

我所教的学生中，有许多人成为了中国与日本的桥梁，为促进中日友好做着巨大的贡献。

中日政府间的关系时冷时热，偶尔产生摩擦，这种不稳定的状态的确存在，但我相信，我们民间的交流不会转冷，并且会如流淌的水一般绵绵不绝，一浪推一浪。

两年前的夏天我患了场大病，住进了上海市的医院并接受治疗，所幸已康复并活到现在。那个时候我就下定了决心，为了学生，为了中日友好，我要更加地努力！

人各有各的使命。我为何来中国？我是为抱着成为中国与日本之间桥梁的目的来到中国的。这个志向直到现在也没有改变。

现在已是我在上海生活的第15个年头，我想再次回到原点，将最初的志向贯彻下去。

作者简介：

泽田依子（日本籍）毕业于日本创价大学，现担任上海外国语大学日本文化经济学院教师。

五、印象篇

LA CHINE EN FOLIE (A COUNTRY IN A FRENZY)

Boris Lopatinsky

I couldn't resist the reference to Londres[1]. Perhaps it's telling me on some level that my life is not so different from that of Albert Londres. Of course, we set out on our respective journeys for different reasons. Nevertheless, we share a thirst that is similarly unquenchable: to explore

---

1 译者注：此文章标题沿用了法国作家阿尔贝·隆德雷斯（Albert Londres）的书名。

the world. The China that Albert knew was in constant flux. Of course, there is not much more one could expect from the world in 1925. China at the time was nothing to envy.

When I arrived in Changchun I had just bid a not unpleasant farewell to Hong Kong. That city, full of life and bustle, seemed bubble-wrapped in her outlying islands that resembled a green-ash wedding ring box. Hong Kong had once effused the wisdom of stability, and was the place to be for international finance. Nowadays, however, Hong Kong has bartered away its soul of little factories, lines and workshops in order to worship the god of consumerism, service and everything superficial, for a liberal but pitiful society, which devours every Boson particle of people's dreams and turns them into one-time goods that can be thrown away at any moment. When I was a little boy, I dreamed of visiting Aberdeen, the famous port full of junks, fishing boats and its legendary restaurant in the bay. Imagine my astonishment when I actually laid eyes on Aberdeen. The place resembled neither Verne's description in *The Tribulations of a Chinaman in China*, nor that in *Le Monocle Rit Jaune (Agent Monocle Forces a Smile)*. Everything I had dreamed about, from junks and fishermen coming back with their hoards of treasure, to the deafening musical cacophony of the market, were gone. Everything was replaced by faded yellow, gloomy buildings, not without a layering of concrete — perfectly standard, of course. But what more could you expect from those bankers? They would readily admit that their goal is to make everything on earth exactly the same. I think you will understand why I had no regrets or bitterness when I left Hong Kong. I followed my instincts and slipped away to northeast China.

There is an old Chinese saying — yes, you know how the Chinese like their sayings, pearls of ancient wisdom and other proverbs — but what nation on earth doesn't have such expressions? These phrases appear to come ready-packaged, ready to be used anytime, anywhere. Wasn't it in China that I came across an "unusual" such pearl so surprising and yet so quintessentially British: "An apple a day keeps the doctor away." Apart from constipation, I really can't imagine what good an apple can do. But what was I about to say? Oh, I remember: "You only know the meaning of 'wealth' once you come to Guangdong. You think you know the meaning of 'knowledge', but that's before you visit Beijing. Only a visit to Changchun will teach you the true meaning of 'cold'."

I arrived in that mythical place (northeast China, not Changchun). For me, it was like having a dream come true. I finally got there, to a place where anything was possible. However, no matter whether it is in the past or the present, does anyone actually know Changchun? No. To the French, who grew up reading *Le Monde,* China stopped at the boundary of Beijing. Of course, there are other places like Hong Kong, Guangzhou, Shanghai, or Macau, the latter famous for its casinos. North of Beijing, nothing to report. You might as well ask a monk to detail the mysteries of married life as ask someone from Europe, from the West, to point out Urumqi, Hohhot or Yinchuan on the map.

There I was, stood on the tarmac at the half-military, half-civilian airport in Changchun, which people say was the last capital of the last emperor. The most fanatic fans of Bertolucci's *The Last Emperor* love to repeat this. I think Bertolucci painted a rather idealized version. However, the place was also, as Albert Londres said, a nest of thieves, place of warlords, and where Aleksandr Kolchak met his end, soon to be followed by Freiherr von Ungern-Sternberg. We have to admit that the lure of Eastern gold and silver was irresistible, but northeast China will always remain a land resistant to foreign occupation, peaceful to those who come in peace. The Russians were routed at Port Arthur; the Japanese arrived arrogantly attempting to subjugate the proud people of the north, but were repulsed like so many before them, mourning their dead, as we mourn the misery of the world. It seems one cannot arrive in northeast China with arrogance, without losing something in return. For me, that something was my certainty.

Changchun is claimed by everyone to be a place of "eternal spring", which is entirely true. Unlike Kunming, which enjoys temperatures of 20°C throughout the year, Changchun's "spring" is different and difficult to imagine. In September, skies are clear and temperatures reach 25°C; at the end of the month, the temperature drops to 5°C. But, autumn is autumn. Nature, however, loves to play tricks: the foliage is just as green as ever. There is not a hint of brown, not one conker. By mid-October, the temperature falls to minus 20°C. Welcome to northeast China, where you will find that while the vegetation is covered in snow in early winter, it will catch you by surprise and remain green. In a letter to his rather worried parents, my colleague Sebastian, a professor by occupation, wrote simply, *late autumn, lovely late season, the temperature just dropped to minus 20 degrees.* Imagine the look on their faces! Sebastian was from Nantes, where the temperature never drops below 5°C. I could find no better words to express it than his "lovely late season". The following year, the temperature at night fell to minus forty-three degrees. Nevertheless, we got used to it in the end.

The weather brought back memories. In Hergé's *The Blue Lotus,* how come it didn't snow? Poor Tintin wasn't wearing much — how did he survive in such a cold environment? Perhaps we will never know. No matter what, I was living in the same place as Tintin had so many adventures. Unlike *Tintin in the Congo*, Tintin in *The Blue Lotus* really cared about the local people.

There I was measuring the length and breadth of the northeast, from Changchun to Shenyang, from Shenyang to Lüshun, and from Lüshun to Jilin, and so many other amazing places, like Mt. Changbai. There is a brand of cigarettes with the same name, that I liked for a long time. Then, I discovered Tumen, a border town beyond which lies mysterious North Korea. Standing on the high bridge looking down, Tumen seemed much nicer than the famous Yanji, as the only city in China with only one Chinese restaurant — all the rest are owned by Korean Chinese. I couldn't resist popping up to Vladivostok.

Vladivostok is a special place. In winter, the sea freezes. One afternoon, I bravely decided to take a stroll on the ice. It wasn't slippery — it was even rough in some places. But there I was, understanding how Jesus felt when he walked on the water. I saw the ice was dotted with holes dug by fishermen, but I didn't see anyone that day. Island after island towered in front of me, at once close by and distant. I walked on and on... It began to grow dark, with the sun beginning to set. It was time to go back. It was only then that I realized how far away I was from solid ground. I had better hasten back, otherwise the darker it got, the more dangerous and lethal the cold would get and I wouldn't be able to see anything — I might even fall into one of the holes. I walked faster, but the beach still seemed so far off. I didn't feel the cold because I was moving quickly. I realized how stupid it was to go so far and not watch my watch. However, after I had gone some way, I saw Sebastian, flirting with his future wife, Irina. I didn't want to be the third wheel. Later on, we went to the Paris Café, where I ordered an espresso. The coffee shop had a really homely atmosphere; late that afternoon, many people seemed to have had the same idea all at once to go there and enjoy the warmth. The women were beautiful and there was a lot of potential for a good time to remember long afterwards. Even if, like Albert, I had all these temptations to stay in Vladivostok, I still wanted to go back to China — the country was more like my second home.

Other than the temperature, there isn't much difference between Changchun, Guangdong and Nanhai. These cities are a hive of activity, life, ideas, plans and dreams. The Chinese who I passed in the street want to be the next Rockefeller or Rothschild. However, there can only be one king. The uncertainty of the market means that money is changing hands quickly: yesterday's princes might be paupers today and then billionaires the day after tomorrow. I thought I'd gone back to the era of the golden boys (poor puppets and novices controlled by those experienced puppet-masters), the big corporations, and financial sharks. They cannot simply be treated as "the initiated" however, because they would be hurt. They had no sense of regret, or morals; they would get the biggest bang for their buck from you — they would bleed you dry. These puppets live up to the moniker of "butchers". They are skilled with the knife and cleaver. Slicing, chopping and smashing the lives of men, indiscriminately. When they walk by on the red carpet, boundless desire flashes in their eyes: this is the new model for people to follow, a dream already come true. But how many of those who were on top seven years ago are still there? None. Every one of them has been drowned in the flood of the subprime crisis, swallowed up by bigger fish. Still, I have no fear that the bigger fishes' turn will come eventually. They will become the food for the pack of ravenous dogs of economic development — what sociology clinically calls "cycle theory".

Albert is always at my side. I follow in his footsteps, amazed, admiring, ecstatic. I am enraptured. I recognize just how great a frenzy China is in.

The country is covered in cities that are mushrooming all over the place.
As Blaise Cendrars put it so well:

At the end of the year 1911

A band of Yankee bankers

Decided on a location for a town

Far out west — at the foot of the Rockies.

Before a month was done,

A new city had sprung up

Without a single house, yet connected by three lines

To the national rail network.

Workers flocked from all over;

By the second month,

Three churches had been founded;

And there were five theatres doing a roaring trade.

Around a town square where only a few old trees remained,

The rest had become a forest of girders,

Day and night, the steady beat of hammers and cranes

Clamoured day and night

The sighing of the machines

Steel skeletons of houses thirty floors high

Began to take shape,

Their towering walls mostly made of brick

With aluminium plates plugging the huge long gaps in the steel structure

In a matter of hours, buildings of reinforced concrete are poured

In the Edison method.

Because of some superstition,

The investors didn't know what to call this city,

So a raffle was set up by the

City's biggest paper with a handsome award

For the winning name.

The paper itself needs a name.

China is undergoing the same frenzy. It's like an infectious craze, where anything seems possible. We can try to do anything we want. Architects have cottoned onto their moment of opportunity: with relish they pull down old buildings in order to build better ones. They raze everything to the ground in order to wipe the slate clean of a past that doesn't match their aesthetics. Everywhere sends up a cacophony; cranes are constantly swivelling, lifting cement or breeze blocks. Here, metal chassis of buildings echo with the sound of hammering; there, by the side is a forest of bamboo scaffolding and metal pipes. These buildings are surrounded in a green gauze; observers can only get a glimpse of its shape. The plague, however, isn't confined to construction. The same thing is happening in business. There'll be somewhere that yesterday was a bookstore and today sells gaudy bling. After tomorrow, it will be a fruit store. Who knows what the future holds, but I can say fairly certainly that the China I used to know — the one that Jilin represented to me — has given way to a China that I do not recognize. Everything seems to be moving in an unpredictable direction, like ever deeper abysses, but there is one thing that *is* for certain: like Albert Londres, I know that however frenetic China of the present may be, China is still the eternal China.

About the Author:

Boris Lopatinsky (French) graduated from the School for Advanced Studies in the Social Sciences (EHESS) and teaches French at the French department at SISU.

炫目中国

Boris Lopatinsky（法国）

我忍不住用阿尔贝·隆德雷斯[1]的书名作为我这篇文章的标题。也许它正以某种方式告诉我，我离隆德雷斯的人生并不遥远。当然，我们踏上各自旅途的缘由不同。但我们拥有共同的、并且难以满足的渴望：发现这个世界。隆德雷斯的中国充满变化。的确，在1925年，我们哪里还有别的期待？那时的中国没有任何值得外人羡慕之处。

我抵达中国长春前，正不无欣慰地与香港说了再见。香港，这座充满活力又喧嚣的城市，被包围在由一座座岛屿形成的灰绿色首饰盒里。那是一座曾经较为宁静的城市，是国际金融中心。但如今，她的小工厂、小作坊已被一个以消费、服务为主的浮华社会取代。那是个自由却可悲的世界，她让一切事物披上了相同面目，她吞噬了每个人的梦想，让它们变成了可随手扔掉的一次性产品。小时候，我梦想着去香港仔，一个以平底帆船、渔船和海湾一家风格怪异的餐馆而出名的港口。但当我真正看到香港仔时，我是多么惊讶啊！它一点也不像凡尔纳在《一个中国人在中国的遭遇》或者《德洛玛的苦笑》（*Le Monocle rit jaune*）中描绘的那样。我幻想中的帆船、满载而归的渔民们、市场的喧嚣声，统统消失不见。这一切都被土黄色的、阴郁的、混凝土造的建筑替代，中规中矩。但是对于那些商人，你还能期待什么呢？金融业的目标难道不是同化这个世界吗？现在，我相信你们能理解为什么我离开香港时，心中毫无悔意或苦涩。我相信直觉，没有过多思考地就赶赴中国东北。

1　译者注：阿尔贝·隆德雷斯（Albert Londres, 1884-1932年），法国记者。

中国人喜爱熟语、箴言和成语。世界上哪个民族没有自己的熟语呢？它们是现成的，随时随地都适用。正是在中国，我碰到了一句"非典型"熟语，但它却别具英国风味：一天一苹果，医生远离我。除了能带来便秘，我真不知道苹果还有什么好处。回到熟语上来……啊，比如还有：只有到了广东，才会知道什么是富有；只有到了北京，才知道什么是底蕴；只有到了长春，才知道什么是寒冷。

我到了那里，那个神秘的地方——不是长春，而是中国东北。对于我来说，我的梦想成真了。我终于到了那里，一个一切皆有可能发生的地方。但是无论是现在还是过去，有谁了解长春呢？没有人。对于我这个读《世界报》长大的法国人来说，中国就等于北京。当然，还有其他城市，比如香港、广州、上海或以赌场出名的澳门。没有人会提及北京以北的地方。让一个欧洲人，或者一个西方人在地图上指出乌鲁木齐、呼和浩特或者银川，还不如让一个和尚指出夫妻生活的奥秘。

我下了飞机，踏足在长春半军用半民用的机场跑道上。我记得有人告诉我，这是中国末代皇帝的最后都城，正如贝托鲁奇的狂热影迷们津津乐道的那样。但事实上贝托鲁奇在电影里理想化了这座城市。然而，隆德雷斯曾经说过，这里同样是匪徒麇集之地，军阀混战之地，高尔察克[1]殒命之地，继他之后，罗曼·冯·恩琴-斯坦伯格[2]亦命丧于此。要知道，东方的黄金和白银确实让人垂涎，但中国东北一直坚决反抗外敌入侵，而和善意之人和谐相处。俄国人在亚瑟港溃败；日本人趾高气昂地想征服并控制这片土地上生活的骄傲

1　译者注：高尔察克，全名为亚历山大·瓦西里耶维奇·高尔察克（Aleksandr Vasilyevich Kolchak，约1874年-1920年）。俄罗斯军事家和北极探险家，海军上将。
2　译者注：罗曼·冯·恩琴-斯坦伯格，全名为弗莱尔·罗曼·尼古拉·马克西米里安·冯·恩琴·斯坦伯格（Freiherr Roman Nikolai Maximilian von Ungern-Sternberg，1886年1月22日-1921年9月15日），俄国男爵、白军将领，外蒙古统治者（1921年2月3日至7月6日），外号"血腥男爵"。

的北方人，但他们不得不一次又一次铩羽而归，哀叹着日本士兵的阵亡，就像我们现在哀叹这个悲惨的世界。似乎到东北的人们都不得不收敛自己身上的傲气。在那里，我也失去了原有的笃定。

人们说长春是春城，这完全正确。但她和昆明不同。昆明全年的温度永远维持在20℃。而长春则有另一番春城景象，并且这种景象难以想象。九月时，天气晴好，气温25℃；到月底，温度急剧降至5℃。毕竟秋天就要有秋天的温度。但大自然极爱开玩笑：植物依旧绿意盎然，而不是一截又一截的枯木。十月中旬，气温便降到零下20度。如果你们在东北，会吃惊的发现初冬之后，那里的植物在冰雪覆盖之下仍显绿色。我的同事塞巴斯蒂安老师回信给他忧心忡忡的父母时写到：今年秋末，气候适宜，气温刚降至零下20度。想象一下他父母的表情吧。他们是法国南特人，那里最冷时的温度不低于5℃。我实在找不到比他更好的表达了，那的确是一个"气候适宜的秋末"，因为第二年，晚上的温度是零下43度。但最后，我们总算适应了这极端的天气。

这让我想到一个问题。在埃尔热的《东北》（*Le Dombé*）[1]里怎么就不下雪呢？可怜的丁丁穿得那么少，他是怎么在那寒冷的气候中生存下来的呢？这将会成为一个不解之谜吧。无论如何，我也在丁丁历险的地方生活过。与《丁丁在刚果》中不同，《东北》一书中的丁丁对当地的中国人充满了热爱。

我不断丈量着东北，从长春到沈阳，从沈阳到旅顺，从旅顺到吉林，还有其他那些让人讶异的地方，比如说长白山。长白山也是个香烟的品牌，我有很长一段时间十分喜欢这个牌子的香烟。后来我又到了图们市，一座与神秘朝鲜接壤的城市。站在高高的桥上鸟瞰，图们看上去比著名的延吉市要好得多。延吉市是唯一一座只能

---

1 译者注：埃尔热的《丁丁历险记之蓝莲花》，因内容涉及中国东北，本文作者将之称为《东北》（Le Dombé）。

找得到一家中餐馆的中国城市，市里其他餐馆都是朝鲜族所开。我稍作停留之后，便前往符拉迪沃斯托克。

符拉迪沃斯托克是一个特别的城市，那里的海面冬天会结冰。一天下午，我勇敢地决定在结冰的海面上行走。冰面并不光滑，甚至在某些地方可以说坎坷不平。不过我还是踏了上去，心里想象着耶稣是如何在加利利海上行走的。冰面上到处都是渔民挖凿的洞，但是那天我并没有看到渔民。我的对面矗立着一座又一座的小岛，那么近，又那么远，我走着，走着……天色渐晚，夕阳西下，该回去了。直到这时，我才意识到我离陆地有多么远。必须赶紧回去，否则天色越晚，寒冷越甚，看不见路，还有掉进渔洞的风险。我加快了脚步，但陆地似乎还很遥远，我并不觉得冷，因为我走得很急。我意识到走那么远而不看时间是多么愚蠢的行为。走了很长一段路之后，我看见了我的朋友塞巴斯蒂安，他正在跟他未来的太太伊丽娜甜言蜜语。我不想打扰他们。后来，我们来到了"巴黎咖啡馆"，我点了一杯特浓咖啡。这里的气氛友好而亲切，那天傍晚，人们似乎不约而同地走进了那个温暖的地方。女人们很美丽，在这里度过的美好时光应能成为日后难忘的回忆。和隆德雷斯一样，这里有众多的理由吸引我留下来，但是我还是想回到中国，那里更像我的第二故乡。

除了温度以外，长春、广东或是南海之间其实并无差别。这些城市都热力四射，充斥着活动、生机、想法、计划与梦想。与我擦肩而过的中国人，他们想象着成为新的洛克菲勒和罗斯柴尔德。但是真正发大财的人毕竟是少数。市场的不稳定性导致财富流转迅速，昨天的有钱人，也许今天变成了穷人，后天又成了亿万富翁。我仿佛回到了雅皮士时代，幕后黑手操纵可怜的木偶，巨头企业垄断市场，盘剥者让企业大幅裁员，这群人早已经验丰富。但我们决不能认为他们深谙此道，否则他们会感到不快。他们没有悔恨心，没有道德感，会从你身上获取最大利益，会榨干你最后一滴血。他们坐实了"屠夫"的名号。他们是刀与砧板的信徒，打磨、切割，随意地剁碎了千万人的命运。他们就像明星，无论走到哪里，他们的眼睛里都闪烁着无尽的欲望之光：这是新模式，那是已实现的梦想。但是这些人中，有多少人能维持其地位？没有。他们被次贷危机的海啸淹没，被比他们更加庞大的商业大鳄吞噬了。但我很肯定，永远会有更大的商业大鳄出现。他们会变成滋养经济发展的养料，在社会学中，我们把这种现象称作"循环理论"。

隆德雷斯一直与我同在，我追寻他的足迹。我惊诧，我赞叹，我入迷，我陶醉：一个充满活力的中国，城市像雨后春笋那样涌现，正如布莱斯·桑德拉尔[1]说的那样：

1911年末

一群美国金融家

决定在远西地区

落基山脚下

建立一座城镇

第一个月尚未过去

三条国家铁路已贯通

依旧无人居住的新城

劳动者蜂拥而至

到第二个月

三座教堂拔地而起

五座剧院人流如梭

在一个广场周围

留下了几棵树

剩下便是金属梁的森林

锤子，绞车

1　译者注：布莱斯·桑德拉尔（Blaise Cendrars），法国作家。

日夜不停的节奏

机器的喘息

三十层建筑的钢铁骨骼

已开始排成线

墙通常由砖头砌成

钢铁梁的缝隙

由简单的铝片填充

根据爱迪生的方法

人们可以用几个小时

用爱迪生模式浇灌出钢筋混凝土的建筑

出于某种迷信

人们不知道如何命名这座城市

于是便在本城最大的报纸上

设了一个奖品丰厚的征名比赛

而这份报纸也尚未命名。

中国正在经历同样的疯狂发展，如飓风一般。一切皆有可能，人们可以实现他们心中任何所想。建筑师意识到了他们的机会，他们满心欢喜，拆除旧建筑，设计新建筑。他们将不符合自己审美的老式建筑统统夷平。处处喧嚣，起重机不断吊起水泥、焦渣石。在这里，击打声不断回响在金属屋架之上，建筑四周是竹制脚手架和金属管的"森林"。绿色纱布笼罩着整栋建筑，人们只能隐约窥见它的形状。但这样令人炫目的发展不止于新建筑拔地而起，商业领域亦是如此。昨天的书店今天就变成了一家销售廉价首饰的小店；后天，又变成了一个水果店。没有人知道未来会发生什么，但我可以这样说，我曾经了解的那个中国，吉林所代表的中国，已经让位于我不甚了解的中国。一切似乎正朝着不可预测的方向发展，令人难以捉摸，但有件事十分确定，就像阿尔贝·隆德雷斯一样，不管中国的发展如何变幻莫测，她都是那个永恒的中国。

作者简介：

　　Boris Lopatinsky（法国籍），法国高等社会科学学院（EHESS）毕业，上海外国语大学法语系教师。

A CULTURAL STORY ABOUT CHINA

Celine Veronique Garbutt

The looking glass

It is the southwest of England, and we are in the mid-eighties. I am about fourteen.

Life is good.

Milk is delivered in glass bottles with foil tops by a milkman in a small van, to the door step. The colour of the foil top tells us if the milk is whole or semi-skimmed. If you are not quick enough, the milk freezes in winter, which is quite amusing.

Coffee is instant and an espresso is something you find only in the local Italian restaurant.

The telephone is a large plastic affair, with a dial punched with holes for the fingers to turn it for each digit.

There is no internet, no email. A letter to France takes a week. To Malaysia two weeks, if sent airmail. There are special stickers for airmail and social networks are pen-pal clubs.

I live in a big house with a small terraced patio out back, and I have my own room with a door, which I can shut to lie down on the carpeted floor looking upwards and out towards the sky to watch the plump and round clouds racing with the wind in the evening, or guess a warm day as the sun gradually melts away a morning mist.

I feel very ordinary.

My town is a typical English town. In the mid-eighties there are no foreigners, and just being from a neighbouring village is enough to make you stand out.

I am half French. And my mother makes my clothes. I look different. I smell different. I eat different. I talk different at home. Therefore, at school, I am different. I am foreign.

At school, the teacher asks me to leave the classroom because I smell of garlic.

Naturally, I form a taste for different things. And I like drawing and art.

My grandfather has a friend who deals with oriental antiques. His son is a friend of my father's. At home there are catalogues with beautiful paintings, sculptures, stones and calligraphy.

I begin to fall in love with the idea of China.

Then someone gives me a book about Chinese, and I find some old manuals on Chinese language at my other grandparents' house in the attic.

And my grandmother brings me flash cards from San Francisco... I find an old book about the country, I read *The Small Woman* by Alan Burgess, which has pictures of China.

Like a young girl who discovers her "husband to be" through a faded old photograph tainted by the fashions of the time, I discover a romantic image of China through jaded books.

But Chinese is not common in the eighties; there is little promise of work. It is a subject for scholars, and you cannot survive with it. And I am not a scholar. So I study something else at university.

However my inner compass still points East.

Through the looking glass — the real China

Thirty years later in 2012, I arrived at SISU and fate led me to Professors Chai and Zhang from GIIT. This was the "real" China, so different from what I had imagined and grown to believe.

At first it was the honeymoon; everything was new, and exciting.

Then gradually, reality settled in.

But a certain charm remains, like the weathered face of someone you love.

Today a letter actually takes longer to get to Europe than before, but we have email, the internet and mobile phones.

Being away from my family is not the cut and dried separation it used to be, though flights still last as long.

What I appreciate the most today is the passion to get on with life that can be felt almost everywhere. And a constant supply of simple food at any hour of the day.

It is also apparent here that it takes all sorts to make a world — and here you can be that sort: no one will mind if you are wearing pyjamas feeding pigeons in the park. Other people go about their singing and exercise oblivious to the world around them.

This would be totally unheard of in the West — and probably considered inappropriate behaviour! Whereas here there is less inhibition.

Like any coin, I remind myself how important it is to remember there are always two sides. I think what helped me the most in adapting to life here in China was to arrive with a blank page and be open to a new way of life.

In this way there is less inclination to compare but rather one to try to understand, and take things for what they are and how they are. In other words, it has helped me look at the coin from the other side.

Happiness is made up of the small pleasures in life ☺ and so far in my life here in Shanghai I have found many to choose from.

About the Author:

Celine Veronique Garbutt (British) graduated with a Master's Degree on Conference Interpreting from ISIT, Paris, and now teaches at the Graduate Institute of Interpretation and Translation, SISU.

一则关于中国的故事

Celine Veronique Garbutt（英国）

镜子

那是八十年代中期的英格兰西南部小镇，我大约14岁。

生活无比美好。

牛奶被装在用锡纸封装的玻璃瓶中，由送奶工驾着小车送到每家每户门口。通过瓶盖锡箔的颜色，可以判断牛奶是全脂的还是减脂的。有趣的是，如果你在冬天未能及时将牛奶取进屋的话，牛奶很快就会结冰。

咖啡都是速溶的，你只能在当地的意大利餐馆买到现磨的咖啡。

电话是一个很大的塑料物件，手指需要插进拨号盘上的一个个小孔拨打号码。

那时候没有网络，没有电子邮件。寄封信到法国需要一个礼拜，寄封航空邮件到马来西亚则需要两个礼拜。航空邮件需贴上特殊的邮票，社交联络主要是通过笔友俱乐部。

我住在一栋大房子里，屋后有一小块空地。我拥有属于自己的房间。锁上房门，我可以躺在地毯上仰望天花板；透过玻璃，我可以看到形态各异的云朵与风赛跑，或者在温暖的时候看初升的朝阳驱散清晨的薄雾。

我的生活非常平常。

我居住的小镇是一个典型的英国小镇。八十年代中期，那里没有什么外国人，就算是邻村人的出现也会引人瞩目。

我有一半法国血统。我妈妈亲手给我做衣服，我的衣着打扮、身上的气味、吃的东西、在家里讲的语言都与众不同。正因为如此，我在学校和其他人显得不一样，像一个外国人。

在学校，老师曾经因为我身上的大蒜味而让我离开教室。

自然而然地，我喜欢的东西与别人慢慢变得不同。我爱上了绘画和艺术。

我爷爷有一个收集东方古董的朋友，他儿子是我爸爸的朋友。我家有很多作品目录，里面充满了美丽的绘画、雕塑作品、石头以及书法。

我开始爱上了有关中国的事物。

恰好，有人给了我一本描写中国的书，我也在爷爷奶奶的阁楼里找到了一些关于汉语的陈旧小册子。

我祖母从美国旧金山给我带来识字卡，我找到一本很旧的书：艾伦·柏格斯写的《小妇人》，里面有描绘中国的插图。

就像年轻姑娘通过泛黄的老照片选定自己"命中注定的丈夫"一样，这些陈旧的书开启了我对中国充满浪漫的幻想。

但在八十年代，学习汉语并不常见，因为很少会有工作机会。它仅仅是一门供钻研的学科，你不能指望靠它养活自己，况且我也不是一名学者，所以，我在大学选择了其他的专业。

但我内心的指针始终指向东方。

来到镜中世界——了解真正的中国

30年后的2012年，我来到了上海外国语大学高级翻译学院，命运使我结识了柴教授和张教授。这才是真正的中国，和我从小想象和理解的完全不同！

对我而言，起初就像蜜月一样，所有的事物都是新奇的，令我振奋。

然后，理想回归了现实。

但中国的魅力犹存，就如同爱人那饱经风霜的脸庞一般。

今天邮寄一封信到欧洲所花的时间甚至比以往更久，但我们有了电子邮件、网络和移动电话。

和我的家人分离也不再像之前那么心酸难过，尽管旅途的飞行时间一样长。

每天最令我感动的是，生活的激情无处不在。全天候都有充足的简单食物供应。

显而易见，这里生活着各种各样的人，你可以随心所欲地生活：没人会介意你穿着睡衣在公园喂鸽子，公园里其他的人则在旁若无人地练嗓子、锻炼身体。

这在西方是闻所未闻甚至可能被认为是不恰当的行为！而在这里，人们却不会觉得奇怪。

就像硬币都有两面一样，我提醒自己任何事物都有其两面性。我认为帮助自己适应中国生活的最大诀窍，就是将过去变成一张白纸，对新的生活方式抱有开放的心态。

这样我就不会总是去比较，而是更多地试着去理解和接受事物本来的样子。换言之，这能帮助我更好地看到事物的另一面。

幸福由生活中点点滴滴的小乐趣组成。就目前在上海的生活而言，我已经发现了很多人生的乐趣。

作者简介：

Celine Veronique Garbutt（英国籍）毕业于巴黎高翻学院会议口译硕士学位，现担任上海外国语大学高级翻译学院教师。

YOU HAVE COME TO THE RIGHT PLACE[1]

Jeroen van de Weijer

Dear foreign teachers, President, dear Deans, Staff, Colleagues,

My name is Jeroen van de Weijer. I am a teacher of linguistics in the English College. I just started my fifth year of teaching in SISU. Time has certainly flown by.

When I first arrived, four years ago, I had no idea what to expect. And still, every day that passes brings new surprises. If there is one thing that I learned during those four years, it is to learn to embrace those surprises. Embrace what is new, value the change, adjust yourself, adapt.

You have come to the right place. SISU is a wonderful university.

1　注：本文为Jeroen van de Weijer教授在2013年9月上海外国语大学外国专家迎新见面会上发表的致辞。

As teachers, we are enormously lucky to engage in the miracle of passing on knowledge, passing on understanding. There is no more fulfilling profession, I think you will agree, than that of the teacher. No greater satisfaction than knowing that a class has been well taught. No greater happiness than finding that students have advanced a little bit in their understanding, in their humanity.

And all of this happiness can be found right here, in SISU. In the past four years, I have found our SISU students are very bright, very eager to learn more, they can be extremely hard-working and they value their experience as a group of students.

Walk around on Hongkou or Songjiang campus and see all their activities, their dreams, their sense of community. Enjoy the privilege of being part of that community.

You have come to the right place. Shanghai is a wonderful city.

The city is of course, enormous, but don't let that deceive you. Shanghai can be small-town in its own charming ways. For instance, the lady selling *jianbing* outside has been the same for four years, and her basic technique of making *jianbing* has not changed for thousands of years.

If you buy her *bing* once, she may or may not have a friendly "nong hao" for you. But if you buy from her a few times, she will quickly know how you like your *bing* — normal spicy or very spicy. And if you buy from her regularly, she will soon know all about you that you can offer to her in Chinese.

I am joking of course, but my point is, relations start small. You cannot take on Shanghai as a whole, so start with your neighborhood and explore. Enjoy your residence in the city, and it has much to offer.

You have come to the right place. China is a wonderful country.

Among nations, China is increasingly at the frontier when it comes to education in general and higher education specifically. Whereas other countries have had to cut back on education in economic hard times, China invests an increasingly large percentage in education and research.

This emphasis on education of course has a tradition of centuries, and is apparent everywhere. A friend told me that his daughter had to take three written examinations and two oral ones to enter a particular school — that school in fact was a kindergarten.

So the emphasis on education may be a little heavy-handed sometimes, but I am sure this will balance itself it out in the years to come. Meanwhile, SISU benefits from its success as a university in which research, teaching and application of research in teaching go hand-in-hand.

The university is constantly renewing itself, updating, for instance, by introducing more technology into the classroom and by hiring the best expertise to teach our students. That expertise, dear colleagues, is you.

Enjoy your education environment, talk to your colleagues, find out what's going on in other departments, because something is always going on.

And, finally, you have come to the right place — for food. We are guests at the SISU Foreign Experts Building tonight, so I wish you all a happy evening and a good dinner. Enjoy your time at SISU and make the best of every day.

Thank you. *Xiexie dajia.*

About the Author:

Jeroen van de Weijer (Dutch) specializes in the field of linguistics. He is now a professor and doctoral supervisor from the School of English Studies, SISU.

你们选择了正确的地方

耶鲁安（荷兰）

尊敬的外国专家们、校长先生、院长、工作人员以及同事们：

我名叫耶鲁安，是英语学院语言学教师。一转眼，今年已经是我在上外任教的第五个年头了，真是时光飞逝啊！

四年前刚来的时候，我对周围的情况还几乎一无所知。然而，过去的每一天都给我带来了新的惊喜。如果说过去的这四年我学到了什么，那就是学会迎接惊喜。迎接新的东西，珍视变化，调整自己，学会适应。

你们选择了正确的地方——上外是一所优秀的大学。

作为教师，我们何其幸运，可以投身于传播知识、散播理解的奇迹。你们应该会同意我的观点：再没有比老师更有成就感的职业了；再没有比用心教学生更快乐的了；再没有比发现学生在理解能力和为人方面取得哪怕是小小的进步更欣慰的了。

所有这些快乐的感觉你都能在上外领略到。过去四年来，我感到上外的学生聪明刻苦，渴望学习，并且珍惜他们作为学生的身份和经历。

若你在虹口校区或是松江校区漫步，看看学生们组织的活动，感受他们的梦想，他们的集体意识，你也会享受到成为这集体中一份子的快乐。

你们选择了正确的地方——上海是一座精彩的城市。

当然，这座城市很大，但你不要被这个现象所迷惑。上海也能以其独特的方式像一个小城镇一样迷人。比如说，门口卖煎饼的阿姨在那里已经四年了，而她做煎饼的手艺是千百年来流传下来的老手艺。

如果你第一次买她的饼，她也许会友好地对你说"侬好"。若你在她那里多买几次，她就会立刻记住你喜欢的口味，如微辣还是重辣。如果你定期买她的煎饼，她很快就会对你的一切了如指掌。

开个小玩笑。我的重点是，建立关系是从点滴开始的。不要将上海作为一个大的整体来看，你应该从你的街坊四邻开始熟悉起来，珍惜在这座城市度过的时光，你可以获得很多。

你们选择了正确的地方——中国是一个伟大的国家。

目前，中国在各项教育事业（特别是高等教育方面）的投资已跃居世界前列。当其他国家在经济不景气的情况下纷纷削减教育开支的时候，中国在教育和科研方面的投入却在大幅度上涨。

当然，中国对教育的重视已经有上千年的传统了，这点在所有地方都可以看得到。一个朋友告诉我，他的女儿必须要通过三门笔试和两门口试才能考进一所学校，而这个学校实际上是一所幼儿园。

这种对教育的重视也许有一些头重脚轻，但我相信在未来的日子里，它会逐渐取得平衡。与此同时，上外作为一所大学，也受益于研究、教学和实践的齐头并进。

上外始终致力于开拓创新，与时俱进。比方说，教室中引进了更多的教学设备，聘请优秀的专家们来给学生上课。而这些专家，就包括你们。

享受这里的教育环境，加强与周围同事的交流，了解校园内的最新动态，因为周围总是有很多事情在发生。

最后，你们选择了正确的地方——因为这里的美食。我们今晚是外国专家楼的客人，祝大家用餐愉快，度过一个美好的夜晚。祝你们享受在上外的时光，让每天都充实度过。

谢谢大家！

作者简介：

Jeroen van de Weijer（耶鲁安，荷兰籍）研究领域为语言学，现为上海外国语大学英语学院全职教授、博士生导师。

DISTANT LAND, BRAND NEW HORIZONS

Murat Elmali

I arrived in China on Thursday September 11th 2014. Everything concerning my arrival had been taken care of in advance. When I landed, my student Wu Yi was there to meet me at the airport exit. SISU even arranged a minibus to take me to my accommodation — the Foreign Experts Building. My flat consisted of two bedrooms and a living room, all very nicely decorated. There was pretty much everything a whole family needed to live there. Before he left, Wu Yi told me the location of the nearest supermarket as well as a few other places I might need to go, and then we took a trip to get some urgently needed supplies. After Wu left, I was all on my own. What was I supposed to do? I had traveled abroad a few times before coming to China, but my longest trip had only been ten days, and I had always been with friends. However, I was to spend almost a year in China. Apart from Han Zhimin and Wu Yi, I knew nobody, and I couldn't speak a word of Chinese. On my first night in China, I turned on all the lights in the flat in order to feel a bit less lonely.

The next day, Han Zhimin accompanied me to the Hongkou campus, and introduced me to Grace Leung and Christine Zhang at the International Office, with whom I had previously been in contact via email. They are both really friendly and helpful. As I was sorting out all my procedures, they patiently went through each step I needed to take.

That Saturday I went to Shanghai International Travel Healthcare Center (SITHC) for my visa medical. The day after that, SISU organized a meeting for all the new international faculty, so I went along. The meeting was in a spacious, square hall. There were only four or five Chinese present, including Grace and Christine — it felt at that moment like a conference room at the United Nations.

Of course, my story will not recount the events of every single day like a diary: the details above are the "adventure" of my first arrival in China and life over the first few days. These are all normal things that happen when someone arrives in an unfamiliar country.

Actually, there wasn't any great change in how I lived over the ensuing days. The next Monday (September 15th) I began teaching classes. From that day onwards, I began shuttling between the university — to the school minibus — and back home. Naturally, I also took part in some other events, but because I'm not a big socialite, liked my new flat, and had a lot of work to do, I didn't have that many chances to get out and see the city.

Over such a short period of time, for someone who had almost no knowledge of the city, I didn't really have much of an impression of Shanghai. That's why I want to talk about my understanding of the university, Shanghai and China.

However, for someone newly arrived from abroad, I was just beginning to form my opinion of the place. It might be a bit one-sided or premature to talk about my impressions of the country. It might be more appropriate for me to talk about the subject in May or June 2015, allowing me to provide a changing perspective on China for comparison.

Impressions of SISU

My first three months at SISU have given me a basic understanding of the Chinese university system. Firstly, I have learned from my students about the immense difficulty of gaining admission to university in China and how much more difficult it is to get into a good university. This is very similar to the situation in Turkey.

From my very first lesson, I noticed that my students were all very well brought up. In Turkey, I had previously taught at primary, junior and senior high school, and university level, but I had never seen such disciplined and respectful students. At first I thought only SISU was like this. It was only after I began to teach part-time at Shanghai University that I realized this is what sets *Chinese* students apart. When I first noticed this, I found it rather odd. At the university where I taught before, the students also respected their teachers; but in China, often we have to encourage them to participate in classroom discussions. Respect for one's teacher is certainly commendable, but students need to ask questions, comment and explore issues further. Sometimes, tricky questions can actually push the teacher to prepare better and make class more diverse and fulfilling.

I should add, about the university, that not only the teaching staff but also the office staff recognize the importance of international education. In this respect, we can see the efforts China is making to strengthen international relations. However, in order to understand what China is really like, you have to see it for yourself.

Impressions of Shanghai

To any questions about Shanghai, my instinctive reaction is to reply, "Shanghai is an international city." Even though during my first three months in the city, I couldn't speak any Chinese at all, I still got by just fine, even feeling that I wasn't in a foreign country. Perhaps after a longer period when I understand Shanghai better, I will change my mind. If I want to understand China and its culture better, I have to work harder.

Impressions of China

The biggest stereotype in Turkey about China is of cheap, low-quality

Chinese products. What's more, people think that the problem exists in everything from everyday supplies to the automobile industry. Although this view is on the decline, it still exists in the minds of the Turkish. I think the biggest reason for this prejudice is the lack of understanding between our countries; perhaps, also, the amount of trade cooperation between China and Turkey hasn't reached the required level yet. On the other hand, closer ties between our nations will make these prejudices disappear.

I myself am a witness to this process — I had similar prejudices in the past. Although I have not been in China for long, since I came to Shanghai my prejudices have been replaced by wonder. If China's other cities are even half as developed as Shanghai, then the Turkish have no idea what China is like. Nevertheless, this reflects the fact that although China is developing, it hasn't put enough effort into promoting itself. Perhaps in the not too distant future, people will have a better understanding of China.

Of course, there are many other aspects to China worth talking about. In order to discuss them, I would first have to go out and gradually learn about Shanghai, and China. All this requires time. Now, though, winter is approaching so I'm even less keen on venturing out. If I get the chance perhaps I will take a trip to some of the cities around Shanghai. That way, I will have an opportunity to better understand China and the Chinese.

<u>About the author:</u>

Murat Elmali (Turkish) graduated with a doctorate in Turkish language and literature from Marmara University. He is currently an assistant professor at the University of Istanbul. In September 2014, Elmali became a visiting professor teaching Turkish at the School of Asian and African Studies, SISU.

遥远的国度，全新的天际

Murat Elmali（土耳其）

　　我于2014年9月11日（周四）来到中国，一切有关事项在我抵达之前就都替我准备好了。一下飞机，我的学生吴奕就在机场出口处迎接我，上外还安排了一辆校车把我送到了我上海的家，也就是上外的专家楼。我的新家两室一厅，非常漂亮，在这里基本上有可供一个家庭生活所需要的全部东西。吴奕同学在临走前告诉了我附近的超市位置和其他一些我可能需要去的地方，然后我们去超市买了一些急需的日用品。吴奕同学走后，只剩下我一个人，我该做点什么呢？虽然在来中国之前我也有几次出国的经历，但是最长也只有十天，而且我的朋友们一直都和我在一起。但是，我要在这里待将近一年的时间，除了韩智敏老师和吴奕同学，我谁都不认识，而且我一个中文词都不会。在中国的第一个夜晚，我把房间所有的灯都打开了，希望可以排解一下孤单的感觉。

　　第二天，韩老师陪我去了虹口校区，带我认识了之前通过邮件联系的国际部的Grace和Christine老师。她们都是非常和蔼、乐于助人的老师。在我们办理手续的时候，她们把所有的细节都耐心地一一告诉了我。

　　周六我和吴奕同学一起去了上海国际旅行卫生保健中心办签证体检，周日上外召开了本学期新聘外国专家的集体会议，我也出席了。会议在一个宽敞的方形会堂进行。会场内加上Grace和Christine老师总共也只有四五个中国人，那一刻我觉得自己仿佛身处联合国的会议室。

　　当然，我的文章不会按照这样一天一天地记叙，不然就变成了简单的流水账。我前面所讲述的只是刚到中国的"冒险"和头几天的生活，是任何一个人到了一个陌生国度后，都会发生的一些平凡的事情。

事实上，我的生活在接下去的日子里也没有多大的变化。周一（9月15日）课程开始了，从那一天起，我开始了学校——校车——家之间三点一线的生活。当然我也参加了一些其他的活动，但鉴于我不是一个特别热爱社交的人，加上我很喜欢这个新家，手头还有许多需要完成的工作，因此我没有很多机会参观游览这座城市。

在这么短的时间里，对一个几乎没参观过上海什么地方的人来说，当然印象也不会太多。所以我仅仅想谈一下我对学校、这个城市还有这个国家的了解。

但是对我这个初来乍到的人来说，我对中国的看法才刚刚形成，可能略有偏颇，要谈论印象可能还为时过早，也许到明年五、六月份再来谈这个话题更合适一点，届时你们可以对比一下我对中国看法的改变过程。

大学印象

在上外的这三个月让我对中国的大学体系有了初步的了解。首先，我从我的学生那里了解到，在中国考上大学是相当不易的，要考上好大学就更为困难了，这和土耳其的情况很相似。

从我在学校的第一堂课开始，我就观察到我的学生们都有非常高的素养。我曾经在我的国家担任过小学、初中、高中和大学的老师，但是从来没有见过这么有纪律、这么尊敬老师的一群学生。起初我以为这只是上外特有的一个现象，直到我最近开始在上海大学兼职任教，我才发现这是中国学生特有的现象。最初看到这个场景时，我也感到有些奇怪。在我原来的大学里，学生对老师也非常尊敬。但是在中国的课堂上，我们需要时不时提醒学生加入课堂讨论。不得不说，对老师的尊敬是值得赞许的行为，但是学生也需要提问、评论和探讨问题。有时，学生在课堂上为难老师也能促使老师更好地研究备课，使课堂更丰富多彩。

对大学，我还想补充的一点是，在这里不管是教学队伍还是管理层，都很重视国际化办学，在这一点上，大家能看到中国在加强对外关系方面的努力，但是要了解真实情况，必须到中国亲眼看一下。

城市印象

如果要我回答任何一个和上海有关的问题，我的第一反应一定是"上海是一个国际化的城市"。尽管在最初来到中国的这三个月来我一句中文都不会说，但我依然过得很好，甚至我都没有感觉到自己生活在国外。或许过一段时间，等我更好地了解上海以后，这个看法会产生变化。如果我想更多地了解中国和中国文化，我得更勤快一点。

中国印象

我们国家对于中国最大的偏见，就是中国产品价格低廉、质量不佳，而且从日用产品到汽车工业都是如此。尽管这个看法有逐渐减少的趋势，但是在土耳其人的脑海里仍存在这个偏见。我认为产生这个偏见的最大原因就是两个国家互相不了解，或者是两个国家之间的经贸合作没有达到应有的水平。反之，两国之间关系的提升可以使这种偏见消失。

对于这一点，我本人可以作为见证人，之前我也有这样的偏见。虽然我来中国的时间并不长，但是一来到上海这座城市，我的惊叹就取代了这种偏见。如果中国的其他城市有上海的一半发达，那可以说土耳其人根本不了解中国。但是同时，这也反映出中国在发展的同时还不够重视对自己的宣传。也许在不久的将来，大家对中国的认识都会有所提高。

当然，对于中国的其他方面，还有很多值得谈论的。要谈这些，我需要先走出自己常住的地区，慢慢了解上海，了解中国。这些都需要时间。而现在冬天到了，我更不乐意出门了，或许有机会的话我会去上海周边的城市旅游，这样我就可以对中国和中国人有更进一步了解的机会。

作者简介：

Murat Elmali（土耳其籍）毕业于马尔马拉大学土耳其语言文学博士学位，现担任伊斯坦布尔大学副教授，于2014年9月被派往上海外国语大学东方语学院土耳其语专业担任教师。

CHINA THROUGH MY EYES

Nataliya Tsisar

I. Before going to China: cultural stereotype

Before I went to China, a lot of people would ask me: "How are you going to survive there? We have such a big difference in language, culture, etc." It didn't matter to me at that time since I was using the principle: what is different doesn't mean it is wrong — try to adjust. At that time, my image of China was mostly based on its great ancient culture: calligraphy, poetry, history. I had no clue about present-day China. I was also thinking: "Well, I'm just going for one year. So, my first year in China will also be my last one there." But it's already my third year in Shanghai, and I'm still here, and still enjoying the diversity of this great (in both meanings: size and culture) country.

II. The first period in Shanghai: ways of cultural difference through first impression

Food

During my first weeks in Shanghai, a lot of Chinese were asking me how I like Chinese food, to show that they were concerned for me. That time I thought: "Is it such a food-centered culture?" Later I understood that it's not just the basic need, but that food is just the reason for families to gather. It's a symbol of family life. It's also a time for friends to strengthen their friendship, for colleagues to celebrate their successes, and a time to welcome foreign guests. Food also has medicinal value, and various dishes are taken to combat illness.

Often when you talk to Chinese about travelling they would always recommend some food to try in different provinces of China. So, it also means that food could be one of the reasons to discover a new city or province in China.

Distances

The other thing I was getting used to in Shanghai is distance. Distances seem vast in the city, so it makes me think of Shanghai as a sub-country inside of the country. The expansive distances between other cities and provinces give the impression that China is its own continent and not just a typical country. To travel from one Chinese province to another is like travelling from one country in Europe to another. It takes more time but it allows you to experience the diversity of Chinese life. And travelling to a new place is always exciting.

<u>Language and taxis</u>

Before I went to China I talked to a lot of Chinese in my home city to prepare myself and better understand life there. When I asked about the language, they would tell me that, if you were going to Shanghai, you would have no difficulty with the language since English was widely spoken there, and your survival Chinese was enough. Life in China seemed easy, but not when you are sitting inside your first taxi and telling the driver where you want to go. First, taxi drivers don't speak English. Second, they often don't understand your Chinese pronunciation because they are Shanghainese and speak the local dialect. Only later did I understand the differences in pronunciation between Chinese and Shanghainese, for example, ch-c, sh-s etc.

<u>Nature</u>

My first impression of Shanghai was skyscrapers and buildings, buildings, buildings. This impression is wrong. You have a lot of incredibly beautiful and peaceful, quiet parks designed according to ancient traditions, which is certainly an art form. Here in the park you are able not just to enjoy the nature but also different types of Chinese culture through different generations. It's as if Little China lives in China.

III. After more than 2 years of staying in Shanghai

Nothing seems very different or strange here anymore. Even when I'm returning to Shanghai after travelling in Asia or from my home country, I'm feeling like I'm coming back to my other home.

<u>About the author:</u>

Nataliya Tsisar (Ukrainian) graduated with a doctorate in linguistics from the National University of Ivan Fran Curley Wolf and taught Ukrainian from September 2012 to June 2015 period at SISU.

我眼中的中国

Nataliya Tsisar（乌克兰）

1. 来中国前的印象

　　来中国前，很多人都问我："你要怎么在那里生存啊？语言、文化等方面的差别那么大呢！"当时，这个问题并没有困扰我，因为我相信一条：彼此之间的差异并不代表着谁对谁错——我只需学会适应。那时，我对中国的了解主要是它伟大的古代文明：书法、诗歌和历史。我对当今的中国一无所知。我想："算了，我只在中国待一年，在那里的第一年也将是我的最后一年。"但如今已是我在上海生活的第三个年头了，我仍然在这里。中国地大物博，文化源远流长，中国的多元性深得我心。

2. 初来上海的日子和我所感受到的文化差异

<u>食物</u>

　　在我刚来上海的前几周，很多中国朋友都问我"喜欢中国食物吗"，来表达他们对我的关切。当时我想：中国文化是否是以食物

为中心呢？之后我渐渐明白，吃饭不仅仅是人最基本的需求，也是中国人家庭团聚的方式，是家庭生活的象征，它还能促进朋友间的友情，是同事一起庆功和欢迎外国友人的方式。食物同时还有药用价值，不同的食物能够帮助对抗不同的疾病。

当你同中国人聊起旅游时，他们经常会向你推荐不同地方的特色美食。这也意味着，食物是探索中国地域文化的动机之一。

距离

我逐渐适应了上海的距离。这个城市的地域非常之广，让我觉得上海像是一个大国下面的附属国。每个城市和省份之间的距离是如此之远，给人感觉中国像是一个大陆而非一个国家。当你在中国不同省份之间旅行时，你会觉得像是在欧洲不同的国家间穿行。你需要花很长时间旅行，而这也让你有机会领略中国的多元文化。去不同的地方旅行总是很激动人心的。

语言和出租车

来中国之前，我向很多在乌克兰生活的中国人打听情况，以便更好地了解中国并做相应的准备。当我问及语言时，他们告诉我，如果去上海，语言将不是问题，因为英语在上海运用得非常广泛，我只需学几句基本的中文就绰绰有余了。听上去，在中国生活很容易。然而，当我抵达上海、坐上第一辆出租车并告诉司机目的地时，问题来了：首先，出租车司机不会说英语；其次，他们听不懂你的中文发音，因为他们大多是上海人，讲上海话。后来，我才慢慢理解了普通话和上海话发音的区别，如上海话常把ch发成c，sh发成s等。

大自然

我对上海的第一印象是它的摩天大厦。除了高楼，还是高楼。然而这一印象是错的。这里还拥有很多令人难以置信的、美丽宁静和很有艺术美感的中式公园。在公园里，你既可享受大自然的美景，也可观察到不同年龄层的中国人所代表的不同文化。公园就像一个小的"中国城"。

3. 在上海生活了两年多后……

　　这里的一切都不再新奇和陌生了。即使当我从亚洲其他国家旅游回来或者从我自己的国家返回之后，我都会感到，自己像是回到了另一个家。

作者简介：

　　Nataliya Tsisar（乌克兰籍）毕业于伊凡弗兰柯利沃夫国立大学语言学博士学位，于2012年9月至2015年6月期间担任上海外国语大学乌克兰语专业教师。

SISU INTO NATIONS AND BEYOND

Nicholas David Jackson

*S*ilver dreams lit our way, from near and far,

*I*nto Huangpu we sailed, to view our star.

*S*eagulls of Pudong soared above Jin Mao,

*U*pon-the-sea, our destiny was now.

*S*ounds of every tongue swept us through Hongkou

*I*nto that stream *humaine* of old Malraux.

*S*wayed by the mind and shadow of Lu Xun,

*U*nder his tree grew our East-West fusion.

*S*ongjiang's students rose up to start our day,

*I*nspired us to open up a new way.

*S*un's rays on campus, shining in her pond,

*U*nto us appeared a bridge to beyond.

About the author:

Nicholas David Jackson (Anglo-American dual nationality) graduated with a doctorate in history from Syracuse University, and now teaches at the School of English Studies, SISU.

作者简介：

Nicholas David Jackson（英美双重国籍）毕业于美国锡拉丘兹大学历史学博士，现担任上海外国语大学英语学院教师。